B

Table of Contents

sew them back on for Jesus ...
The hippie dome

Life in small town America ... 1979-1991

#$%&* Stoplights!!!!... The big time is where you are at ... Fear
not ... Another piece of straw for the camel's back ... Give the kid
a break ... Fake it 'til you make it ... Please leave a message at the
beep ... Roaring past the harbor ... Tortoise and the Hare ... "L"
word issues ... Marital advice 101 ... D'oh ...
  You're welcome

Second Wind ... 1993-2013

A new beginning ... Support the troops ... To thine own self be
true ... You're a good man, Charlie Brown ... Do what you can
... Find a sheep ... Fred Astaire Syndrome ... 21st century Shake-
speare ... Karen ... Time to go home ... I saw the light ... Deal me
in ... What a wonderful world ... Mirror, mirror on the wall

The final lap around the schoolyard ... 2015-2019

New pair of glasses ... Cancer didn't turn me into the Buddha
... Clueless white guy from Bellingham, Washington ... Grade
yourself on a curve, (and pass/fail in certain areas) ... Some-
times all you need is a mom ... Save your breath ... I never met
a man I didn't like ... Will Rogers, (or a woman, revised by Steve
Morse to reflect current times) ... Enough Already ...
You have two ears and one mouth ... Don't be Al Capone ... I'm
not really a morning person ... Don't trip going down the stairs

Retired life ... 2020-...

FOMO NO Mo' ... Look, Papa, look ... Damn it ... Where are my
yearbooks? ... Who is this guy? ... You should have listened to
me 30 years ago ... Life is long ... Make the coffee every morn-
ing ... Standing in the pouring rain holding a leash ... What, me
worry? - Alfred E. Neuman ... Happiness in the time of Covid
(This would make a great movie title!) ... I got hacked today ...
I stepped on a matchbox car in the middle of the night ... Grab
your backpack

Dedication

I'm dedicating this book to my wife Laketa, who loves me and is always there for me. She has inspired me with her kindness, patience, and humanity. I also ask her forgiveness for the 75,000 times I said, "What?", when she asked a question while I was writing this book.

I am also dedicating this book to my daughter, Lianne, my son, Joel, and my grandson Cruz, all of whom I love to the moon. I wanted to leave them a few stories and thoughts. I didn't know it would become a book when I started.

Finally, I want to dedicate this to the many hard-working educators I had the pleasure to work with for 39.5 years. They loved me and accepted me while I grew and when I made mistakes. As Sigmund Freud said, "How bold one is, when they know they are loved." They allowed me to take risks and become a better person in my own unique way, while showing up daily for the challenging job of school principal.

MY STORY

Hear me out

R. Eric Thomas, author of "Here for it, or how to save your soul in America" writes, "Every story, whether truth or fiction, is an invitation to imagination, but even more so, it's an invitation to empathy." .... I am worthy of being heard and you are worthy of hearing my story."

I love telling stories. Any relative, friend, or even casual acquaintance can confirm that as the gospel truth. I was thrilled when I met someone who could keep up with my verbal pace. Then I could just relax and chatter away without having to constantly remind myself to make sure I was giving my friends a chance to get their two cents in. Whenever my wife, Laketa, climbed in the car after dinner with friends and said something similar to, "Andrea can outtalk you!", I was always fine with that. It helped keep me in check without as much effort on my part.

I am also curious by nature and literally almost dying to immediately know everyone else's "story" when I meet them. I'm like the commercial, "Enquiring minds want to know.", or an I-phone that is seeking for network connections every time I enter a room.

Every single person in this world has a story and each of them want someone to hear them and know them. People want to be loved and accepted for who they are. As an elementary educator for forty years, I always made time to stop what I was doing to listen to the kids. I wanted to get to know the "real" them. I shared a fair share of my own anecdotes with them, also. They never complained, because they loved getting me off track hoping the bell would ring before we got back to the lesson.

As Mr. Rogers says, "When I say it's you I like, I am talking about the part of you that knows that life is far more than anything you can see or touch or hear."

As I neared retirement age, a number of people encouraged me to write a book of advice for school administrators. I was a reasonably successful principal for 24 years and worked in public schools for 39 years. I decided to give it a shot. After about six months of attempting to get much on paper, I realized I didn't have much advice for principals, or anyone else for that matter. Being a principal, like life in general, is a tough gig. Good luck! I have complete confidence that you will figure it out yourself like I did!

Another friend has been encouraging me to write a little every day about "whatever" and see what happens. As an avid storyteller, I thought this was a better suggestion and just started writing my story. As I wrote, I realized I might have learned a few things. Maybe some of the tales will resonate with you and you might pick up a nugget or two. Just like Paul Simon and Julio, I spent a lot of time down in the schoolyard, almost sixty years as a student or educator, so a lot of the stories are based in schools.

Many of the stories I remember like they were yesterday. I can visually see the people's faces and viscerally feel the emotions of that encounter. It's like this scene in Back to the Future II...

Marty: It's like I was just here yesterday!

Doc: You were, Marty, you were. Amazing, isn't it!

I hope you enjoy my story and that a few of the anecdotes resonate with you. While writing, I found the self-reflection healing and it was cheaper than paying a counselor. I realized that while I'm still pretty much the same old Steve, I'm also an entirely different person. When I faced the problems that popped up going through life, I realized that most of them were outside of my direct control. My only hope of surviving and making this life livable was to recognize and deal with my part in the issue. Most problems could only be solved by changing myself, not trying to control everyone else.

I selected the photo of myself as a toddler trying to change a tire because it seems like a metaphor for most of my life. I often felt like I had no idea what I was doing but dove into the task before me anyway. Most of the time someone came alongside me to help me finish the job. In this case, it was my dad.

I like this take on the serenity prayer. "God grant me the serenity to accept the people I cannot change, the courage to change the one I can, and the wisdom to know it is me."

If you have suggestions, comments, or a story you want to tell, email me at stevemorse5072@comcast.net. My enquiring mind is dying to know your story!

I changed the names of most of the people (and all of the students) in this book but left a few with their permission. I used the names of my family members, and my old friend, Dana.

Walking the track

I was working at my computer in my office when I heard Michael ask the secretary if he could see me. She asked what he needed and asked if she could help him.

"No, I just want to hear the story about pulling his friend in the wagon again."

She chuckled and let him know that this time was set aside for me to finish some essential paperwork and told him to come back another time. True to form, I hollered around the corner, "Send him in!". There was no way I was going to miss an opportunity to tell my stories one more time! I enjoyed the retelling more than the kids liked hearing them.

My poor secretary probably was worried the central office was going to call her demanding that paperwork soon. She would end up getting the heat if payroll was late. Within a few months, there were about half a dozen coming by to hear stories all the time. I think she finally gave up and just sent them in, once I proved to be reliable about getting my paperwork done.

When I was the principal at Sunnyland Elementary, there were two kids who wouldn't follow adult directions and often refused to go to class. The bathroom, wandering the halls, or off campus were their preferred locations.

My best strategy for noncompliant kids was story telling. When a kid is mad, they generally won't talk, but they love listening to stories. My wayward elementary days were coming in handy!

I had zero interest in trying to corral them in my office while they tore posters off the wall and tipped over desks and chairs, so I invited kids for a walk when they were angry, rather than trying to drag them into the office. I don't ever remember being turned down. Their bodies craved movement and they felt trapped inside.

As we strolled the track, I told them stories about when I was a kid, especially the ones where I was in trouble in school. They loved my classmates' nicknames. Luckily, I messed around enough as a kid that I never ran out of material. They listened and tried to act all tough and angry for a few minutes, but I could see them grinning and they cooled off within a lap or two. They pitched in with their own stories and soon we were both laughing. These two boys became some of my best friends, and I didn't need to purchase a gym membership that year. They came by to visit me before and after school and almost every lunch or recess period.

Some of my stories needed the adage, "Do as I say, not as I did." When several of my high school mentees got involved with the law, Nancy suggested that maybe I share fewer personal anecdotes with them. To be fair, I tried to choose mentees that were struggling, not the kids needing help on their Harvard essay, so I don't think my stories were the main issue.

A Prayer

"Holy One, you have given us the gift of story in our lives, ways of understanding who we are, ways of making sense of our world, of finding meaning and knowing how to respond to all that happens in our lives. Please show us where our stories fall short or are too narrow, where they exclude rather than include, where they divide rather than unite. Help us to see where a story we live out of may go amiss of what is real, where it allows us to escape becoming whole, where it lets us live comfortably in fear.

Fill us with your story, the story of unity and compassion and love. Fill us with images that energize us and give us hope and lead us to the fundamental truth that you have tried to teach us all along: we are all one. Amen."

--Judy Cannato, Field of Compassion: How the New Cosmology Is Transforming Spiritual Life
H/T Cindy Pleis

ELEMENTARY, MY DEAR WATSON ... 1960-67

What a nice little boy...hee-hee

Go, Spot, go. Run, Stevie, Run.
The room was stifling hot and the small windows were doing no good at all. I was squirming in my seat and watching the second hand click by on the clock. I still hadn't learned to sit still for five seconds, even though I was in the third grade. I was listening intently for the signal to line up.

My jacket was on and my desk clear. When the teacher excused us to line up, I raced for the door, being just cautious enough to not get sent back to my desk. When the bell rang, I shot out of the room like it was the start of the Kentucky Derby and hit the pavement running like mad.

I had been following this routine of racing the five blocks home for several days. For some reason, a group of about six boys decided I needed a good beating and made certain I was aware of it. I was a fast kid and they hadn't caught me yet. I began to think they would never catch me, and my anxiety went down half a notch after the first couple of days. I just had to stay focused on being first in the line to go home. I would have no chance from the back of the line.

I had my usual half block lead when suddenly my gut felt like it was going to explode. I must have eaten too much for lunch. I darted up the sidewalk to a house where I saw a lady in the window and pounded on the door. She opened the door, and I begged her to let me use her phone, while the thugs stood in the street and watched. She kept repeating, "Get off the porch. I don't want any trouble," before shutting the door on me.

I rested another few minutes on the stairs of the porch, recognizing I would need my stamina to make it the final two blocks home. I pretended I wasn't too worried and feigned boredom while waiting until I thought they were in a semi-relaxed state. When they appeared to be losing focus, I leaped up and sprinted diagonally across the lawn, leaped the flowerbed, and onto the street. I was hoping my superior speed would save the day. Alas, they had a better angle and pounced. A couple of guys held me for the leader to begin the beating. The bashing only lasted for one punch, as the first blow landed solidly on my Adam's apple and I went down immediately. I couldn't draw a breath.

I don't know if I was out for a few seconds or not, but when I looked up, they were freaking out and wondering what to do. I heard a kid whisper, "I think we might have killed him." Another guy was slapping my face like they did in the cowboy movies and saying, "Snap out of it, snap out of it." I sat up, mostly so that idiot would quit slapping my cheeks. That stung!

They picked me up and fireman carried me to one of their houses. No adults were in the house, so I started worrying again. He asked if I wanted cookies and hot chocolate. We shot pool and enjoyed our snack. I pulled out the only tool in my toolbox and decided to win the group over with my humor and story-telling. Soon they were all howling and invited me to walk to school with them the next day. They told me to meet there early, as they shot a little pool, drank hot chocolate, and had a donut before leaving for school. They liked to start the school day about fifteen minutes late, as they preferred to miss the attendance and pre-game stuff. That sweetened the deal even more for me. I had to decide if I would rather race home fearing for my life every day or start the day eating donuts and drinking cocoa. It took about a tenth of a second to respond. "See you tomorrow at eight o'clock."

Mom was thrilled to see that after dragging my heels about going to school for the first several years, I was leaving an hour early every day. With five wild kids, she probably didn't take the time to wonder why.

Now I got to be the wolf instead of the rabbit, chasing some poor soul home every day. It was chase or be chased. I felt bad about this, so I made it my undercover mission to help the victims as much as possible. I lingered near the back of the pack and rooted for the kid to get away. When a kid was caught, I usually waited about thirty seconds and then stepped forward to announce, "He's had enough. I think he's learned his lesson." I was never quite sure what the great lesson we were imparting was, but for some bizarre reason, as soon as I said, "He's had enough," they stopped hitting and kicking. In retrospect, I think they didn't really want to extend the beatings either. They were like a dog chasing a car and didn't know what to do if they caught someone. I told myself I was at least doing some good in the world by getting them to stop quickly. It helped my guilt for being part of this group a little bit.

Sometimes I feel like I've been running my whole life. Always looking over my shoulder. Always afraid I will stumble, and the wolves will be upon me. Life has been more challenging than I anticipated. In the meantime, all these experiences were preparing me. I didn't realize at the time how much my own school experiences would impact my work as an educator.

Kindergarten Hoodlum

Standing in front of the class, holding my kindergarten teacher's hand, I strained my neck to see what she was going to say. "Class, I want to introduce the new boy to you. He's not a very nice boy. Don't laugh at him or pay attention to him."

I couldn't believe my ears. This is one of the dozen or so moments that I remember as if it happened yesterday. If my memory is correct, I immediately thought, "If you think I was bad before, just wait now." I declared war on her and continued my skirmishes with teachers for the thirteen years of K-12 public education. I had been suspended for general messing around and because I never stopped talking. I wasn't malicious. I was just having fun. However, the teacher thought my enjoyment of school was disrupting the education of the other students.

Over the years, I found myself in a fair amount of trouble for screwing around, but I never bullied anyone and was reasonably respectful to the teachers. I generally stopped doing what I was doing when the teacher told me to stop and didn't argue much. Unfortunately for me, I could only stop, sit still, and listen for a few more minutes before I started moving and talking again. I'm sure I would have been assessed for ADHD if I were in school after 1980. Instead, I was just repeatedly told what a naughty boy I was.

Being told I was naughty always made me feel bad. I thought I was a nice kid. I was kind to everyone I met and had a million friends. I was a lot of fun and made everyone laugh. I couldn't wrap my head around why the teachers believed I was so terrible. My mom seemed to agree though, so I began to own that reputation. I suppose I didn't sit still or shut up much at home either.

I'm 64 years old now, and still can't hold still for more than a few seconds. My 34-year-old daughter, Lianne, asked me to stop kicking her car seat from the back seat and to hold still while she was driving the other day. I looked over, and my grandson, Cruz, age two, was looking out the window without fidgeting. He has already surpassed my ability to sit still!

After a few days of suspension, the principal let me come back on the condition that I would be transferred to the afternoon class. They were hoping the new group wouldn't find me quite as entertaining. I still have a tough time controlling myself around people who think I'm amusing. Unfortunately, the new group of classmates soon grew to appreciate me, and I continued on my merry way.

This happened 59 years ago, but it remains a seminal moment in my life. I remembered this episode clearly when I ran into little guys and gals that just couldn't hold still when I was in my principal gig. This was one of many episodes that helped to shape my reputation as being able to work well with challenging kids.

Here is the church, here is the steeple, open the doors and see all the people

Sometimes I felt like I spent most of my childhood squirming around restlessly in church. Our family got there about 9:30 Sunday morning and chatted in the foyer after service until 12:30. We went back at 6:00 that evening for youth group and church and didn't get home until 9:00 again. I begged to stay home once in a while to watch "Mutual of Omaha's Wild Kingdom" or "The Wonderful World of Disney". It was rare, but I still recall my excitement when I got to stay behind. We also went on Wednesday night, and once I was in youth group, usually Friday.

It was a Conservative Baptist Church and according to mom we were the only church that had it right. Not only were all the

Catholics, Lutherans, Presbyterians, and Pentecostals wrong, but all the other Baptist denominations. I now consider myself a recovering evangelical fundamentalist. I still hold the Christian faith and attempt to follow the teachings of Jesus, but am trying to leave behind the guilt, shame, fear, and exclusion. As I reflect on my childhood, many of the more fundamentalist teachings of my church harmed me.

However, the teachings of Jesus have had a huge positive impact on my work and quality of life. My 40+ year career in education was based on serving others, helping those that need the most help, accepting people as they are, and showing love by putting others first. The teachings of Jesus weren't the problem. It was my church experience that hurt.

Some of the thoughts running through my head were crazy. I feared that I missed the rapture because I didn't say a prayer right. I even thought things were my fault that I couldn't have possibly controlled. Did I get the flu because I had a bad attitude at Sunday School? Would God punish my family if I messed up? Would the Seahawks lose the game because I skipped church? Even by age six or seven, I knew these thoughts were crazy and couldn't possibly happen, but I couldn't seem to control the obsessive thoughts. When I saw the viral text below from a teenage girl, I laughed out loud thinking my mom or someone in my church might have said something similar to me.

"Sorry, everyone. I just found out that the Coronavirus is my fault. Mom said that God sent it to keep me home on Friday nights."

I haven't attended Sunday Services, other than Easter or Christmas, for about ten years. I became weary with parts of organized religion and gave myself permission to take a sabbatical. I didn't expect it to be this long, but I still feel like I'm growing in my faith and learning about God in different ways. I feel like I'm getting to know myself and not hiding from myself or God. **Richard**

Rohr says that, "Religion is one of the safest places to hide from God".

My spiritual heroes now have shifted from the Franklin Graham and James Dobson crowd to people like Ann Lamott, Richard Rohr, or Gandhi. People who see mystery and ask questions. People who realize they don't know or understand everything. Lamott writes, "The opposite of faith is not doubt, but certainty. Certainty is missing the point entirely. Faith includes noticing the mess, the emptiness and discomfort, and letting it be there until some light returns. Faith also means reaching deeply within, for the sense one was born with, the sense, for example, to go for a walk."

I wrote a poem to the church I attended as a kid to release some of my anger and to offer forgiveness to the people that attended there with me. I can't change my past experiences, so I guess I'll just keep working on my attitude. Unfortunately, that's harder.

Dear Childhood Church
You welcomed me at birth,
Joyfully supported my parents,
I remember sprinting down the halls,
Laughing and chasing my pals,
Playing on the dirt piles when you renovated,

The smiles on the faces of my parents' friends as I whizzed by,
I was loved, accepted, cared for, seen,
Never quiet, always in motion,
Cookies, pies, marshmallow Jell-O, green bean casseroles,
Dunking for apples, eating chips, making friends,
Going to camp,
Sitting around the fire,
Telling stories in our bunks until we heard the wakeup bugle,
Great memories and first girlfriend,
Short lived romance,
Met a lifelong friend,

Learned values that I have lived by,
Servanthood, acceptance of others, helping those needing the most help,
Grace, forgiveness, work ethic, kindness, unconditional love,

Even so, you hurt me,
Waking up in the middle of the night worried I was going to hell,
Fearing I didn't say the sinner's prayer exactly right,
Panicking when I came home to an empty house,
Thinking I missed the rapture,
Scared until someone finally came home to find me crying,

You seemed more concerned about what I believed than who I was,
You were incredibly certain of everything,
Where was the mystery? Couldn't anyone say "I'm not sure,
Questioning or losing my faith was the worst thing I could do,
Backsliding, sinning, listening to the devil's voice,
Couldn't my faith grow, evolve, change?
Were the only two choices losing or keeping,
Is faith a certainty, or an adventure, a journey?
Jesus said you must lose your life to find it,
And that you must become like a child,

In my middle years, I was indignant, mad,
Looking inside my damaged soul,
I had lived in distress from age 5-25,
Repeated the sinner's prayer hundreds and maybe thousands of times,
But never certain I'd said it well enough to get to heaven,
I felt ashamed,
Had lingering doubts and questions,
That I couldn't ask without being judged,

Recently, I was able to let go of my anger,
Like a leaf tumbling from a tree in autumn,
Like water bursting over a mud dam,

I no longer believe I can comprehend everything,
I have left room for doubt,
I cannot live in constant fear,
Nor exclude so many people,

I forgive you, church,
I'm moving on from my disappointment and anger,
You loved me, fed me, cared about me,
Taught me that faith and spirituality matter,
That there is more to this world than material goods and money,
Introduced me to Jesus and his teachings,
Teachings like love, grace, service, putting others first,

Like everything I've experienced in life,
I'll try to keep the good parts and let go of the bad,
Like an orchardist pruning his trees,
Steve Morse 2019

I met a psychic on the sidewalk

Mom and Dad's wedding photo

Laketa and I were strolling down the streets of a small town in Whatcom County when we passed a chalk artist drawing on the sidewalk. She was in front of a store advertising art lessons with wine. The perfect combo. Laketa went in to inquire about the classes, while I relaxed on a bench taking in the rare Northwest Washington sunshine.

The chalk artist kept looking over at me furtively. After a few minutes she asked me if I was religious. I chuckled and said, "I don't know. Depends on what you mean. Maybe a little. Why?"

She told me she was from Canada and had something to tell me, but she had heard that this town was the home of many conservative Christians, and she was afraid that she would offend me. I assured her that I was difficult to offend and encouraged her to go on.

She claimed to be a psychic and said that my mom would not quit bothering her. Mom kept telling her to talk to me every ten seconds, even though she had already informed mom that she didn't know me and didn't want to talk to a stranger in a conservative town. I'm not completely sure I believe in psychics, but I try to be open to mystery. I was dying to hear what mom had to say. Well, not literally dying. When I die, I'll be able to talk to her as long as I want.

The psychic said, "Your mom wants to say that she is sorry." Tears began running down my cheeks immediately. While I wasn't certain the psychic could even communicate with mom, her words touched me deeply. She had a few other details that sounded a lot like mom and said that dad was there, but he was just listening and nodding along. That sounded like dad, too.

I always intuitively believed my mom loved me, but she had such a hard time showing it. She never once said the "L" word and I don't recall being hugged or held, but I'm sure I must have been.

Her apology continues to mean a ton to me. I told my sibs and it means a great deal to them, as well. Not having an emotional attachment to my parents impacted me more than I previously realized. Whether this medium was a fraud or not, I believe that mom would apologize if I could talk to her again, and this encounter left me with a sense of peace that is still with me.

I don't think mom ever loved or accepted herself. The self-acceptance movement didn't seem to be on the horizon yet in the 40's and 50's. She often made statements like, "I'm so stupid. I don't know what's wrong with me. I can't do anything." She seemed angry all the time until she and Dad retired and wintered in Arizona.

Unfortunately for us kids, her inability to accept herself made it difficult for us to feel her love. I knew intellectually that she cared about me, but never felt it emotionally or connected closely. She showed love by cooking, sewing, disciplining, cleaning, and worrying. However, she also left some scars. I reckon we all leave scars on our children. I'm sure I did, too.

I was at an event in my mid-30s on Mother's Day where the presenter asked us to write down the first thing that came to our minds when we thought of something our mom told us over and over. Something that really stuck. I didn't know we were going to have to read them out, so I just wrote the statement I remember hearing the most often. As the people before me shared statements similar to, "I will always love you. You can do anything you want. I believe in you.", I wondered if I should change mine.

I had written, "You are the dumbest kid I've ever met or even heard of." That seemed to be one of her standard lines to me. I admit I was the class clown and would do almost anything on a dare, but the dumbest? I recall looking up at her at age seven or eight and thinking, "If you think I'm dumb, you ought to meet some of my friends. Let's take a walk to the park." Since I was still reveling in my class clown persona, I read my statement and brought the house down laughing.

Looking back now, I think it damaged me much more than I realized. A similar statement still goes through my head at least five or six times a day. I'll miss an easy shot in tennis and say in my head or under my breath, "You are the dumbest tennis player I've ever met or heard of." I'll make a mistake at work and say, "You are the dumbest principal I've ever met or even heard of." It's been a running script for over fifty years. Laketa suggested that instead of laughing about it, I should probably try to stop the loop. It can't be that healthy. So, I have been trying to use that line in my head less often with a little bit of success.

Mom had a tough time knowing how to effectively apply discipline and dad wasn't much help. He had a stressful postmaster job and when he arrived home for the evening, he punched the imaginary time clock on the wall and was officially off duty for the day. Mom often yelled at him for help, but he wasn't too interested, and he likely wasn't sure what to do either, as his father left before he was five. Occasionally he would peek over the top of his newspaper to admonish us to listen to mom.

Mom's primary strategy was to yell a few times and then lose her mind. As we never knew how many yells there would be prior to her losing it, we just ignored her until she lost it and then ran like crazy. At that point, she would come after us with whatever was in her hand. I'm surprised she never had a breakdown

When I was about six years old our church was building an addition. We were under strict orders from mom to stay off the dirt piles after church. I stood watching my friends running around for about two minutes considering my options. I came up with the brilliant win/win solution of playing without getting dirty.

It hadn't rained for a while. As I piled into the backseat, I noticed I was covered with a layer of dust from head to toe comparable to Pigpen from Charlie Brown. Mom turned around in the front seat to announce, "I'm going to wash that suit with you in it." The ten-minute drive home from church passed much too quickly. I pictured how the wash machine spun around and around half-full of water. I knew I could get a breath every third or fourth rotation and was practicing holding my breath. While I was somewhat worried, I assumed it wouldn't be that bad. I knew mom would never do anything life threatening. I also realized I usually deserved whatever I got. You do the crime; you do the time. I was an active enough kid that given the choice, I would choose a quick punishment like a swat or a few trips around a wash machine over a long-term grounding or detention at school. I couldn't handle sitting.

When we got home, mom grabbed a whisk broom and marched me outside. I was beyond relieved that the suit cleaning would be a dry cleaning rather than in the machine! (What is dry cleaning? Sounds like a scam to me, but I'm too lazy to look it up. Although wouldn't a better title to this story be, "My personal dry cleaning?" Anyways, back to the story.) She spun me around and used the whisk broom vigorously to clean my suit. I looked like a cartoon character being whirled around in a cloud of dust. The dry-cleaning event barely hurt, and I felt like I had dodged the proverbial bullet again for about the 500th time in my young life.

Even though I believed my mom loved me, I never developed a close attachment to her. I've often felt bad about that. It doesn't seem possible, but in my memory, I clearly remember becoming somewhat emotionally independent by about seven years old. I felt like I could make my own decisions and didn't really need any input from mom or dad. I was free to ignore most of what they said. I realize teens often feel this way, but I arrived at that destination early.

Three of my four siblings perceived the same hurt and disconnect. My sister, Karen, was hurt by mom and remained emotionally distant throughout her life. After learning she had six months to live, Karen set a goal to make things right with mom before she died. She told mom that she forgave her. Mom couldn't understand why she needed to be forgiven, as all she had ever done was to take care of us and completely give up her own life for us. Karen was extremely disappointed that the rift couldn't heal before she passed.

In the afterlife, I'm sure mom sees thing differently though. I can't imagine her saying, "I'm still pretty mad about you getting your suit dirty in first grade, Steve!" It would seem we would let go of the petty stuff in the next world.

Thanks again for apologizing, Mom. If you are reading my book in the next world, I hope it doesn't hurt you. I recognize that your perspective was vastly different than mine and that you loved me the best way you knew. Also, the more I have reflected through my writing, the more I am remembering all the good experiences and the ways you showed me love.

Mom Came to Visit One Day
You called to me on the street one summer day,
I wasn't expecting to hear from you,
You left this world over a decade ago,
You told me you were sorry,
I wasn't sure it was really you,
Nonetheless, I teared up immediately,

I forgive you for when you fell short,
Parenting was different back then,
You were just trying to help me be a better person,
Somehow, even at five, I knew you were doing your best,
Even when you seemed so harsh,

You had a tough childhood,
The oldest of six on the remote Saskatchewan prairie,
You raised the other five while your parents worked on the

farm,
Relaxation was not in your vocabulary,
Racing around like a pinwheel on a windy day,
You never felt appreciated,
Gave up all your ambitions and interests for us,
Our happiness and success, the only thing that mattered,
The resentment built like a looming storm though,

I'm finally ready to say thank you,
I forgive you,
I'm letting go of my resentment and bitterness,
Now I will try to forgive myself,
And realize I am no dumber than the next person,
We all do the best we can,
I love you; I miss you,
I will see you again someday and let's catch up,
Let's not spend much time on what we could have done better,
Let's start anew.
Steve Morse 2019

I saw a UFO in 1965

Walking home on a clear summer night at the age of ten, I heard a noise above me. The sky lit up and a circular disc stopped directly over my head. I could see the red and green lights circling around and around the disc. It hovered above me for a good ten seconds or more and then zoomed away. It flew past the East Valley Hills in about two seconds. The airplanes we watched leaving Sea-Tac airport took about thirty seconds to get past those same hills. It seemed incredibly real to me, and I raced home to tell my dad.

Dad let me know that I must have imagined it and that was that. I told everyone at school for several days though. About half the kids believed me and told me I needed to call the FBI. The other half thought I was making it up. Enough kids made fun of me that I quit telling my story after several days. I started retelling it a few years later though, and still tell it to this day whenever a conversation turns to UFOs, I still maintain that I saw it. It's one of the dozen or more memories in this book that feels like it happened about an hour ago.

But I'll never be sure. I can't go back in time and I was a ten-year old kid. In my experience, kids imagine all kinds of stuff. Also, there is one other major reason I can't be 100 percent certain to believe what I saw with my own two eyes. (I didn't get shot in the other eye for a few more years, so don't try to catch me on a technicality.)

The other reason is that it could have been the power of suggestion. Prior to seeing the UFO, my friends and I were making our own UFOs out of plastic dry-cleaning bags. We put a dry-cleaning bag over a small pile of charcoal briquets in a little camping barbeque, lit the charcoal, and in a few minutes the bag filled up and took off like a hot air balloon. It was so cool. We did quite a few things involving fire in those days that parents might not let unsupervised nine or ten-year-old kids do now days. In our parent's defense, they weren't really paying attention, so they probably didn't realize the stupid things we were doing.

After three or four unsuccessful attempts we finally succeeded in launching a UFO. We screamed and shouted in excitement for about thirty of the most thrilling seconds of our young lives. Then, the charcoal spilled out and started a small fire on my friend's roof. While this was equally exciting, it ended up putting a kibosh on the whole evening. His dad got the hose, put the fire out, and informed us that we needed to take the plastic off the other two UFOs. We were told to never do this experiment again as long as we lived. He then returned to watch tv and drink beer, his duty done. It's no wonder the Russians beat us on Sputnik. No willingness to take experimental risks in our country.

Now that I understand more about the way a kid's brain works,

I question my sighting, even though it felt real as heck to me at the time. Also, the experience lasted at least fifteen seconds, not just one or two seconds. I still believe it was real but am holding space in my brain for the possibility it wasn't. Who knows?

I've often wondered if I was one of the people abducted, but even the aliens realized I was kind of a numbskull and erased my memory and sent me back. Maybe they wanted someone smarter and more representative of an average human being. I always kind of did things a little differently.

A sixth-grade student in my class in the early 1980s thoroughly believed in sasquatch. His dad was a sasquatch hunter who was quoted in a book about searching for sasquatch. He brought me books, articles, and this cool plaster of Paris footprint. I never once tried to pour an ounce of cold water on his passion. I listened and asked questions. In the back of my mind I was thinking, maybe there really is a sasquatch. I still think there might be one roaming around out there!

Being open to mystery is a much more interesting way to go through life. I'd rather keep an open mind than be the person who informs everyone why something is impossible. The least interesting people I know are 100 percent certain that they know everything about God, politics, relationships, education, and how to live life. In the words of Albert Einstein...

- "Do not grow old, no matter how long you live. Never cease to stand like curious children before the mystery into which we were born."
- "People like us, who believe in physics, know that the distinction between past, present, and future is only a stubbornly persistent illusion."

Richard Rohr adds, "We cannot grow in the great art form of action and contemplation without a strong tolerance for ambiguity, an ability to allow, forgive, and contain a certain degree of anxiety, and a willingness to not know—and not even need to know. This is how we allow and encounter Mystery."

Here's a poem I wrote about seven years ago.

Prove it
I've spent my adult years on the fringe of religion,
Afraid to completely believe or pour myself into it fully,
Skeptical of the fanatics,
Fearing disappointment or being wrong; unsure,
what if it doesn't "work"?
As a young man, I searched for proof,
I studied and prayed,
I stood in the dark street asking for a bolt of lightning,

I've learned proof is hard to find, like a lost key,
I'm less interested now in indisputable proof,
More ok with not being 100 percent convinced,
My eyes now scan for evidence,
The stars, the wind, a storm, a friendship, a sunrise, a seeking in my gut that asks, "Is there more?"
The moon, the sun, the tides, a rainbow
A hug, a kiss, a handshake,
We can analyze and measure many things.
But haven't discovered a measurement tool for.... Awe, love, hope, faith,
My skepticism binds me to the cold hard earth,
But, if I take a deep breath, look, and listen....
Steve Morse 2014

Everything isn't black and white
Before about the age of thirty, I preferred that everything be black and white, but it seldom was. Being raised in a fundamentalist church I always wanted the answer to be clear. One of the

things that surprised me in adulthood, both as a school leader and a human being, was how few situations turned out to be black and white. It also surprised me that I started to like it better that way.

I learned to appreciate my friends and colleagues who were willing to see two sides to an issue. People who think they are always right and aren't interested in considering new ideas are incredibly problematic to work with. Rather than hiring teachers or looking for friends who already knew everything, I found myself drawn to people who ask the right questions and were humble enough to say, "This is what I think, but I could be wrong. What do you think?"

Nels Bohr said, "The opposite of a correct statement is a false statement. But the opposite of a profound truth may well be another profound truth." For instance, if I say it is Wednesday, but it is Monday, that is a falsehood. But, if I say life is full of pain, it is also equally true that life is full of joy.

Barrack Obama recently said, "This idea of purity and you're never compromised ... You should get over that quickly. The world is messy, there are ambiguities. People who do really good stuff have flaws. People who you are fighting with you may love their kids and share certain things with you."

The principal job whacked me upside the head quickly with the reality that the world is messy and there are few easy answers. Many ambiguities popped up daily. I couldn't fix individual people or immediately solve systemic problems. I consider myself lucky if I even have a modicum of control over myself. I had to learn to move forward, doing the best I could at the time, even though the solutions were messy and imperfect. I didn't want to get stuck waiting for a perfect solution, because they often aren't out there.

One thing I am 100 percent certain of; If there is a "next world", I'm sure I will be surprised when I arrive and not say, "Oh, I already knew all that stuff." I'm embracing the mystery!

11ᵗʰ Street peer pressure

Six or seven of us were laying around Stan's house one lazy summer day, when I was in the fourth grade. We were watching baseball and a few of the other guys had a beer from the fridge. I wasn't drinking at the time. One of the guys decided it was time for me to learn to shoplift. They had been shoplifting at the corner store for a few months and wanted me to join in. I wasn't too interested. My fundamentalist background made me fear I would be saving a nickel to spend eternity in hell. I had paper route money, why I would I choose to burn that long?

They put me in one of the guy's older brother's trench coat, even though it was about 75 degrees. It was gigantic and I'm sure I raised suspicion. We walked the couple of blocks to the store. They waited outside on the sidewalk for me to come out and show them what I had taken, ready to cheer me on and congratulate me on my coming of age. I was finally going to be a man. And at such a young age. What a prodigy!

I wandered aimlessly around for a while and kept glancing at the owner. He had always been kind to me. I just couldn't do it. After about five minutes, I came out and informed them that I had decided I would start shoplifting next year. That would leave me plenty of time before I turned 21 to get lots of good stuff. I was hoping they would affirm my decision and tell me how wise I was. Unfortunately, rather than lauding my wisdom, they punched me around a little bit, not too badly, and sent me back in.

I went back in and roamed around again for a while. Walked back out, got batted around a bit more, and returned to the store. They didn't punch me too hard and not in the face, so it wasn't that bad. I didn't even leave bleed or get a bruise. If my memory serves me right, I wasn't too terrified either. Felt like another day at the office. We did lots of roughhousing and I got swats or hit with a ruler on the palm all the time at school.

We repeated this several times, until one of the guys said, "F*** it. Let's go play basketball." I was thrilled but expected to be back there every day for a week or two. I woke up the next morning dreading it, but surprisingly, they never bothered me about this again. Who knew that taking a stand would actually work once?

From the outside, our neighborhood in Auburn, Washington (Town Motto: Better than a poke in the eye with a sharp stick.) looked like the television set for "Leave it to Beaver". Maybe it was a walk in the park for some kids, but it wasn't for me. Laurel, the sister who told me I would be dead meat if she wasn't included in this book, says she had a great experience in the neighborhood and was never hassled.

My peer group was brutal though. The level of bullying was appalling. The kids who were different or didn't quite fit in were called horrible names, and occasionally even punched, kicked and spit on if the teachers weren't looking. As a principal, I had to bite my tongue about a thousand times when parents complained to me about how bad bullies were in our school compared to when they went to school. I wanted to say they were like Mr. Rogers compared to my experience.

I always felt empathy for the kids being harassed. I didn't participate in the name calling or bother them. Even a few of the teachers laughed along and teased the kids that were different, especially after about fifth grade.

By seventh grade, these guys wanted me to finally experience my first fistfight. The decided it was time for me to man up and get in a real knock 'em down punchout. They thought I was a chicken, and they were partly correct. I was kind of afraid, but I wasn't really terrified. We roughhoused and played tackle football every day in the fall. I wasn't that afraid of a bruise or a little blood. In fact, I had recently thrown a knife an inch or so into my foot playing mumbly-peg and mom just put a band aid on and sent me back outside. I didn't shed a tear, but I yelped and jumped around on one foot a lot. Fighting seemed different though. I was just too darn nice. I got along with most everyone and I had no interest in physically hurting someone. Not that I could have hurt anyone anyways. I was so skinny and wimpy that I probably was going to lose no matter who they set me up to fight.

About the same time, I was excited because I had signed up for a six-week exploratory crafts class. Most of my junior high classes sucked. But I was looking forward to making those cool glass balls that knocked against each other on a string. There was a developmentally disabled kid assigned to the class. He had a great smile and was friendly. The crafts teacher didn't pay much attention other than to flirt with the seventh-grade girls, so my "friends" tossed the disabled kid and me into this sizable storage closet shortly after roll call almost every day for a week or two. They said they wouldn't let us out until we fought. I would make a bunch of noise and slam against the door until they would open the door to see if we were fighting. When they saw we were faking, they closed the door immediately.

We ended up in the storage closet enough that I didn't get much done and got an F. Dad mused, "How do you manage to get an F in crafts?" I just mumbled something akin to, "I don't really like crafts.", and he didn't press me too much, thank goodness. These guys weren't big fans of snitches.

My first and last kegger
Every time I hear the song, "Mama Told Me Not to Come" by Three Dog Night, my mind and emotions go back to the final time I stayed overnight at Bill's house in the fifth grade. I can see the smoke filled room, smell the beer and weed (Although I didn't know it was weed at the time.), and see the teenagers nonchalantly spread out all over the room necking passion-

ately. I was huddled in a corner trying to hide behind a lamp, terrified and hoping to go unnoticed. I was staying overnight with Bill and around midnight he got bored at his house, so we walked to his high school aged cousin's house for a kegger. Let me tell you how that ended up being my first and last kegger.

When Bill moved to town, we immediately hit it off. We both delighted in tormenting the teachers, he was hilarious, and we both could play and talk about sports nonstop. In his ten-year old words, "Steve is funny as hell". He was super athletic and popular. I was excited to be his sidekick. For a couple of years, I was strutting around like a rooster, rather than cowering in a corner.

One time we were walking on the other side of town. Bill knew no boundaries and I became pretty familiar with our little town of Auburn. We came upon a group of about six to eight kids playing tackle football in a park. Bill walked right up to them and announced, "It's me and Morse against you guys and we're going to crush you." I was nervous as heck. They didn't look like what my mom would have called "nice boys" to me. I thought they would destroy us by 50 points or decide to beat us up instead of playing football. They had good intuition though. After sizing Bill up for a minute, they said, "No thanks.", and turned around to continue playing their game. Bill calmly took the ball away from them and said, "We'll kickoff first to give you a better chance."

We were ahead about 24-6 when they just left and headed home. I hiked him the ball and took off straight down the field every play running as fast as I could run. They followed me for a while and then figured there was no way he could throw it that far. At that point, he threw it over their heads for another touchdown. I'm not sure why they never figured out he could throw it that far, but it was incredibly fun for a wimp like me to walk in and own the field. You just gotta know the right people.

Bill also liked to fight after school as often as possible. He spent much of his time during the school day on priorities like telling kids he could beat them up and challenging them to fight, rather than the dumb projects our teachers assigned. His would-be opponents usually held out and said "no" if possible, but eventually grew tired of the constant heckling and agreed to fight. I hated the fighting. As I did with the chasing group earlier, I intervened to end the fights as quickly as possible by acting as his manager and letting him know that his opponent had enough.

I "got to" stay overnight at his house several times. I usually felt tentative about it but didn't know how to say "no". He was my best friend at the time. There was smoking, drinking, and arguing there and my parents didn't do any of the three. One time, his cousin got mad at him, and started chasing him around with a butcher knife. He never caught or stabbed him, so all's well that ends well, I guess.

A time or two, we left the house around 10:00 or 11:00 and didn't return until 2:00 or 3:00 a.m. We met up with a bunch of other young hooligans to shoplift, drink, smoke, and go to girls houses to "make out". Since I had quit smoking and drinking in third grade, didn't shoplift, and no girls would come near me, I didn't enjoy these outings and my stomach was in knots the entire time. One time they broke into a building and I stayed out on the street. One of the guys yelled, "Great idea, Steve. You can be the lookout." That wasn't at all what I had in mind, and I broke into a sweat worried I would be going to juvie if the cops came. I never made it to the morning on any of the sleepovers. I never even fell asleep. I called dad at some point each time to tell him I was sick.

Back to the night I spent five minutes at my first and last high school kegger. At some point in our wanderings around town, someone suggested we go to Bill's high school cousin's kegger.

Good grief. We were eleven years old. I fervently prayed that the group would decide they weren't that interested, but that was one more unanswered prayer in my young life. They all enthusiastically consented and off we went. As we entered the room, they grabbed a beer and started looking for girls close to our age. I scanned the room searching for a dark corner where I could hide. My stomach was roiling so much that I was sure I was going to puke. As that wasn't the type of attention I hoped to draw to myself, I self-diagnosed that I was now sick enough to call dad again.

Dad came and picked me up at the address I gave him. It was about half a mile from the house he dropped me at off and almost midnight. The house looked like a scene from the movie "Risky Business" with cars all over the place, music blasting, and high school kids out front smoking and drinking.

Dad sleepily said, "This is the third or fourth time you have ended up sick when you stayed overnight with Bill. Is there anything you want to tell me?"

I slouched lower in my seat and contemplated for a minute or two. I finally replied, "No, nothing to tell you, but I'm not going to do sleepovers for a few years." He agreed that sounded like a good plan. That was an impressive bit of parenting for a dad in the 1960's. Most 60s' dads would have been furious that I woke them up and forced some type of confession out of me. They would have banned me from ever seeing my friends again, which might have resulted in me sneaking around to see them even more. Well done, Dad!

This turned out to be a fork in the road. I began to limit my time with Bill and this group of buddies. They were developing interests that I wasn't interested in at age eleven. We still had fun wreaking havoc on the teachers at school and playing sports at recess, but I'm not sure I ever saw him again outside of school times.

Being scared spitless at a kegger at age eleven, combined with my evangelistic fundamentalist upbringing, kept me from attending keggers all through high school. Since I ran with the non-drinking crowd in Christian College, I'm able to state that I stopped drinking and smoking in third grade and attended my last kegger in the fifth grade. This always piques my colleagues' attention enough to give me one more opportunity to say, "It's a long story, but one day ...

Put me in, coach

I've been a sports fanatic since age five. I was one of the fastest and most coordinated kids in my neighborhood and was a superstar up and down 11th Street. However, I was short and skinny, and never made any inroads in organized or school sports. I ran circles around the football stars in our neighborhood games, but I was lucky if the coaches knew my name on the organized teams.

My early attempts at organized sports were disastrous. My parents were busy parents of five and not too interested in sports. Luckily, my buddy's mom was a PE teacher, so she often signed me up. The first sport I turned out for was Little League Baseball in third grade. I couldn't hit or catch the ball and my speed and agility were little to no help in baseball. Having the attention span of a squirrel was also problematic while standing out in right field. It was the last game of the season, and I still hadn't played in a game. The coaches in the 60's didn't believe in the "everybody gets to play equally, and you all get a trophy at the end of the year" concept that we all seem to ascribe to today. The coach promised me before the final game that "today would be the big day". I would get to go stand out in the field for the last inning if we were way ahead. Looking back now, I think "Big @#$% deal", but at the time I was excited about getting out there in my little uniform. I had spent the whole summer sitting on the bench watching mind numbingly boring games.

The team was warming up, and I was in my usual spot at the end of the bench daydreaming. Suddenly, I was knocked right off the bench backwards and had blood gushing out of my mouth. Our third baseman had tossed a wild throw during warm up that hit me square on the mouth and knocked my front teeth out. We didn't believe in wasting money by putting screens in front of the bench or building dugouts in those days. We were tough and we just took our chances! My neighbor's mom drove me home, and I managed to end my baseball career without even getting into an actual game. If they make a baseball card for me, it will be a photo of me sitting on the bench with no front teeth and blood on my jersey.

Since baseball didn't appear to be the sport I would go pro in, I decided to give football a shot. I tried out for the community league in fourth grade. There was a requirement to weigh 60 pounds and I was a few pounds short. Cheryl and Karen, my high school sisters, took charge. They ran to the grocery store daily for about a week to purchase more ice cream. They forced me to keep eating no matter how full I was. This type of discipline around eating when I'm full has not served me well over 60+ years.

The day of the weigh-in, I was still about half a pound short. My sisters put a few rocks in my pockets and sent me off in my tennis shoes on my sting ray bike. I made the weight requirement by a quarter pound, dumped my rocks behind the bathroom, and was ready to rock and roll. The coaches issued us our uniforms. I was near the back of the line and my uniform was several sizes too big. I could barely see out of the helmet because it flopped around so much when I ran. My knee pads were well below my knees.

For our first activity, the coaches lined all thirty of us up for a race. They announced that the first eight kids would be the running backs and wide receivers and the rest of us would be linemen. As the fastest kid in my school, I strolled confidently to the starting line. I looked down the line and knew I was quite a bit quicker than the other kids I knew from school. I expected to finish first or second. Unfortunately, the cumbersome uniform, the helmet flopping over my eyes with every step, and the fact that I was one of the only kids with no cleats, I finished in 9th place. I knew I could beat every kid there with one more chance, but the coach assigned me a position on the offensive line. Really!!!!!! The smallest, quickest kid on the team, and I'm playing offensive line. I politely asked for a second try but was told in no uncertain terms to never question a coach's decision again if I wanted to make it in little league football. I spent the year getting knocked around in practice by guys double my weight and once again never got to play in an actual game. It was hard to even watch the games from the bench, as my helmet kept slipping down.

It looked like basketball was going to be the sport for me. I set my sights on the NBA and turned out for the North Auburn

Elementary Basketball Squad in fifth and sixth grade. It was exciting traveling around in the teacher's station wagon to other schools. We only had six or seven players, so I knew I would get to play a lot. Alas though, as with all my other coaches, this guy didn't believe in everyone playing. It was much more important to beat South Auburn than to build character or be kind to children. In two seasons, I played about thirty seconds total. I still can see the slow-motion video of a friend throwing me the ball and I'm reaching, reaching, reaching, but can't get there before the ball goes out of bounds. However, it was the only team sport where I got to play. Those thirty seconds were thrilling!

The last week of sixth grade, I had one more opportunity. All twelve elementary schools in town competed in an end of year track meet. We took a bus to the high school track and the stadium was packed with every sixth-grade kid in town. All the racing home after school by a pack of bullies was finally going to pay off! I couldn't wait for the first event. As mentioned above, the coaches weren't too concerned if everyone participated or not in those days, so I was scheduled for a half a dozen events while about 90 percent of the kids just sat and watched, after being admonished to quit complaining and cheer us on.

My classmates convinced me to run in my socks because I didn't have track shoes. This was the first time I had run on a cinder track. For those taking notes, don't run multiple events on a cinder track in socks. Long story short, there were faster kids and my dreams of breaking through the tape at the end were shattered. I think my best placement was fifth or sixth, so no ribbons for me. My homeroom teacher made sure I understood just how disappointed he was. Apparently, I had so much potential.

JUNIOR HIGH SUCKS ... 1968-1970

Moonwalk

It was a sweltering midwestern summer day in 1969. (That would be a great song title!) My family had driven clear to St. Paul, Minnesota, to meet a long-lost cousin of my father's. I was in the eighth grade and this would turn out to be an ill-fated voyage, but more about that later.

I met a suave second cousin who was two years older than I was and a pretty cool cat, as we said in the day. It didn't take long for the two of us to realize that it was too hot to be outside and that sitting around all day with a bunch of old people was not a viable option. Scott noticed a couple of girls about our age on the neighbor's porch. In no time at all, we were heading across the driveway to strike up a conversation. Their parents were at work and they invited us in. About half an hour after our arrival, Scott was necking with one of the girls. The other gal and I sat awkwardly across from each other and attempted to make small talk. We pretended not to notice the other two on the couch about five feet from us. I was waiting to make my big move, but so afraid of girls that we could have been there for another ten years before I ever asked to hold her hand.

My parents sent another cousin over to tell us to hurry back home, as a man was about to walk on the moon! Scott couldn't have cared less at the time. He wouldn't have willingly left that couch if our cousin said the Beatles were performing live in our uncle's living room. I didn't really care either. I wasn't that interested in sitting around a 13-inch black and white tv with 25 relatives I had just met. I probably wouldn't even be able to see the tv. So, we politely declined the offer and sent him back.

About five minutes later, he was banging on the door again. Your parents said you guys have to come right now. We mumbled and grumbled, and Scott told our cousin to let them know we would be back shortly. He necked for a couple more minutes and then we slowly traipsed across the street and stood in the back of the room impatiently. I could only see a fraction of the screen from the back and it was a blurry black and white with an antenna. Finally, Neil Armstrong or whoever the guy was, took his little walk. Didn't seem too exciting to us. The second he took a few steps, we faked a whoop, clapped for a few seconds, and raced back over to the neighbor's house, so I could sit around uncomfortably, while my cousin made out with some girl.

For the rest of my life, every time I saw a movie or heard about the moon walk, I was disappointed that I only saw about a minute of it on a tiny screen from way in the back, and that I wasn't really even paying attention, because I was in a big hurry to get next door. I'd like to say I learned a valuable lesson at age thirteen and became much more interested in living in the moment, but it took a lot more whacks upside the head to learn this lesson.

I'm finally figuring out the importance of taking in the moment when it is happening. I'm attempting to forget about the day to day stuff when there is an eclipse or a big historical moment. I'm trying to clear my mind and thoroughly savor the moments when they arrive. Taming my fidgety restlessness and learning to live in the moment are still major aspirations that are a challenge for me.

For the record, even after we spent about twelve hours a day for the next few days at the neighbors, the other girl and I never even held hands. We barely talked. We just sat there uncomfortably. What a dumb reason for missing a moon walk.

He shot my eye out!

"Dance, partner, dance. Yeehaw", I shouted at Jerry as I rapid fired BBs at his feet. Jerry was Clint's friend and we were playing cowboys at a farm on the western border of Minnesota. This was a few days after the moon walk. I was thirteen, so Clint would have been eight.

The dance scene while dodging bullets was my favorite scene in old Westerns, so I always incorporated it at some point in our games. Clint raised his BB gun and warned me that if I didn't knock it off, he would shoot me. In retrospect, I wish I had taken his warning more seriously. He shot me right in the eyeball! What was he thinking? The Bible said an eye for an eye, not an eye for a foot. If it were me, I would have shot him in the thigh or the chest. Maybe even in the neck, but seriously, an eye? In his defense, I don't think he aimed at all. He just fired away as we both were wont to do.

Blood started streaming out of my eye. As fate would have it, our parents had just left for a leisurely car tour of the beautiful east North Dakota countryside, letting us know they would be back in a few hours. They admonished us to behave and told us that they completely trusted us. I'll never figure that one out to this day. Clint and I were incredibly untrustworthy. Different parenting era, I guess. This was well before the age of cell phones, so they weren't available if we needed them. For instance, what if someone got shot in the eye with a BB while we were playing with our guns.

Luckily, grandma lived with the people we were visiting. I ran into the house to find her. Due to the wisdom she had accrued over a lifetime of living on a farm, she immediately panicked and began giving us a lecture about the dangers of playing with guns. I attempted to listen earnestly and incorporate the knowledge for future incidents involving guns, but I really had a headache and couldn't focus. At least she knew enough to give me a bath towel to hold against my eye during the lecture period. After I thoroughly soaked through the towel, she handed me a fresh one. We were sure lucky she was home.

Clint was running circles around the house crying and yelling, "I'm sorry. I'm sorry." I heard and mentally accepted his apology about every thirty seconds for an hour or so until our parents finally got home. I had a pounding dull headache, but the shock was keeping the pain threshold down. I don't remember groaning and hollering as much as the guys seemed to in the Western's we watched. I think I just sat on the couch holding a towel on my eye with a dull headache.

When they returned, we leaped into the car to head straight to the hospital. Unfortunately, the closest hospital was another hour or two away. We raced along those flat and straight roads, rarely seeing another vehicle. I'm not sure what they saw on their countryside tour. It all looked the same to me in Eastern North Dakota. The doctor wanted to remove my eye. Dad was so upset that he fainted.

When dad came around, He and Mom decided to fly me back home to Seattle, where the surgeons would have a better chance to save my eye than in a rural hospital. I had never been on a plane before and was excited to be able to fly home and avoid the several days of arguing with my siblings in a boiling hot station wagon. This whole deal wasn't turning out all that badly. The doctor in Seattle extracted the BB with a magnet but ended up having to remove my eye a few weeks after that surgery. I had to double the number of surgeries, but at least we gave him a chance to save my eye.

The doctor said if it had been a half inch over and entered the soft part of my temple, I could have been killed or paralyzed. I suppose it was only a matter of time until something comparable to this happened. If my parents had any idea of what we did when we were out of their sight line, they never would have bought us BB guns.

Much to our dismay, our parents took the guns away. We really missed them. We played a lot of army and POW games, often on motorcycles, and it wasn't the same without firearms. One team would escape and the other would hunt them down with BB guns. While both experiences were fun, I preferred to be the guard with the gun chasing the escapee. Clint and his friends were fast and could dart down those trails like rabbits. We had some awesome forests and vacant lots that made great hiding and motorcycle riding areas for many years. It was a kids' paradise.

Lest it seem mean to be hunting down my brother with a BB gun, let me say for the record, it was invariably Clint and his pal, Jeff, who initiated the game. I assumed they wanted to play and wanted to be the American escapees. Personally, it was just as entertaining when I was the escapee. I felt like Clint Eastwood or Paul Newman. However, Clint recently told me that he didn't really enjoy that game, and was mad at Jeff for suggesting it, but he didn't want to feel like a wimp once it had been suggested. Typical male communication skills. Go along with it for years, so you won't have to talk about it or admit you didn't like something. Anyways, I apologize for shooting BBs at you and locking you in a woodshed prison, Clint. However, in all fairness, you did shoot my eye out and we always gave you a good head start. What more could you want?

Losing an eye didn't turn out to be the worst disability. If a villain ever captures you and makes you pick a body part to lose, go for an eye. I definitely wouldn't choose hand, arm, leg, foot, or what an elementary school kid would call your "private part". An ear wouldn't be the worst, but you might look a little lopsided. I think the larger concern we need to address might be, "Why is a villain capturing and threatening you? Did you do something terrible or take out loans with the Mafia? Maybe you need to reevaluate your friendships and life habits."

I have an exceptional Ocularist (glass eye making person) and most people don't even know I have a glass eye. I think the main effect is my depth perception. It makes driving a challenge, so I leave a lot of space between cars and annoy family members by going too slow. It probably effects my basketball, tennis, golf, etc. That makes a handy excuse when I lose a game. Also, I somehow was smart enough not to take it out and try to scare people all the time, so I didn't become even more of a loser around the girls.

Most elementary principals have about a dozen mini lectures at their disposal for the right situations. Not to brag, but thanks to this incident when I was in junior high, I think I was one of the best in the nation at delivering lecture #11, "Don't you realize you could shoot someone's eye out with that rubber band?" My students took my advice to heart once I told my story. I thought about taking this speech on the road to national principal conferences to share my expertise but couldn't figure out how to make the story last 90-minutes to fill the time in a break-out session.

Will you put me in now, coach?
After playing a total of thirty seconds in four years of sports in elementary school, I knew junior high had to be better. I was sure I could make it in football if I had a chance to play a posi-

tion where speed and agility made a difference and a uniform that fit! Unfortunately for me, the two coaches turned out to be the same jackasses that were giving me all the swats in PE. I didn't exactly start with a clean slate.

I got to play quarterback though, which was much better than offensive lineman. The coaches also made a big deal the first day of practice about how everyone would get to play a lot, as this was a school team and education came first. I ran home after the first day thrilled. My sports career was finally looking up. We only had 24-25 kids on the team and football requires 22 starters, so I assumed I would get to play quite a few minutes.

One practice a few kids were missing, so we played a man short on the offensive line during scrimmages. As second-string quarterback, I got sacked almost as soon as the ball was hiked to me a good percent of the time that day while the coaches howled like hyenas. One time, I came out of the pile with my helmet turned around with the facemask in the back. We had to pause practice for a few minutes, so the coaches and players could quit laughing. I left it backwards for a while longer for comic effect and then returned to the huddle to call the play for my next flogging.

Coming up to the last game, the coaches still hadn't kept their promise that everyone would get to play a lot. In fact, I still hadn't entered a game even once. I found this especially disturbing since we hadn't won any games and usually lost by 20-30 points. In fact, we still hadn't scored a single point all season, so couldn't they chance it and let the second-string quarterback play the last minute of a game one time? Did they really think we still might catch up? It looked like I was on track to complete my fifth season of organized sports with less than thirty seconds of playing time total.

At practice on the day before the game, the starting quarterback threw a tantrum and hit the coach in the nose with the ball from about ten feet away. Blood immediately began spurting from his nose and the coach was livid. He flew into a screaming and swearing rage and let the quarterback know that he was through. He would never play another second for the mighty Cascade Spartans. "Morse, you're starting tomorrow."

I was so excited that I could barely sleep the night before. After only playing thirty seconds in the previous four years, I was going to play a full game! The first play of the game I handed the ball off and we gained nine yards. I can still see Mounts ripping through the hole. That was one of our best plays all season. Everyone on the bench was whooping it up. The second play I handed off again and we had a first down. We only had a few first downs total in our previous five games. I was living the dream. I trotted confidently back to the huddle to call the next play.

Suddenly, the starting quarterback was tapping me on the shoulder to let me know he was back in the game. I trotted off the field feeling dejected and ran over to talk to the coach. He assured me that this young man had more than learned his lesson and that was the end of my football career. Way to stick to your principles, coach! Well, at least I got to hand off the ball twice and could say I entered a football game. As that was my last football game in my K-12 experience, I retired with no interceptions as well!

I figured track had to be better, as I had convinced my parents to buy me track shoes with metal spikes! I counted down the days to track season. The first day, the coach asked us who wanted to be sprinters. I raised my hand proudly and informed him that I was the fastest kid at my elementary school. He didn't seem that impressed and for like the 50,000[th] time in my life I wished I could just shut up. He lined us up and off we went. I got a slow start and never made up the ground. I finished in fifth place. He let us know we only needed four sprinters and announced that the rest of us would be running distance. What! R U KIDDING ME! Yet again, no second chances? What the heck. Did all the coaches in our town take the same training? Were they all taught to line everyone up on the first day and never ever, no matter what, give a kid a second chance? Was that against the coaching code of ethics? Would that make them look weak? The die had been cast for the next three years of middle school track. My sprinting career was over less than fifteen seconds after he said, "go". I was stunned, but resilient, as public school had taught me to expect arbitrary and capricious decisions would be made by ex-jocks with extraordinarily little assessment or empathy. A lesson that would help me accept disappointment my whole life. Lucky me.

Another friend ended up in the same boat. We looked at each other and talked about how much this totally sucked. We had no interest in running distance. In fact, we were both rather lazy kids. I asked my parents to call the coach, but they continued the tried and true strategy of saying "That's too bad." while staying out of my business. I must admit, parents in the 60's taught us to be more independent and take care of ourselves, but I was disappointed at the time. Parents today appeal almost every decision and that's way worse for kids in the long run.

The next day, the coach handed us a detailed map of where we were to run. The route took us off campus and around town. He told us what time we should arrive back and sent us off with the admonition to "Run, boys, run". That turned out to be the extent of his coaching for the season. What else could we possibly need to know?

The actual "run boys, run" part of our training turned out to be more challenging than we anticipated. As soon as we were out of his sight, we stopped for a discussion. We were already winded and becoming long distance runners was not something in which we were remotely interested. That craze wouldn't start for another ten years or more when Steve Prefontaine ran for the Oregon Ducks.

After a strategic session, we came up with the perfect plan. There was a donut shop about a quarter of a mile from school. We knew we could jog the couple hundred yards or so to get out of the coach's sight and then walk the rest of the quarter mile. We both had paper routes and access to a bit of spending money. So, most days we jogged until we were out of the coach's sight, walked to the donut shop, downed a couple donuts and a cola each. We watched the clock attentively, walked back until almost in sight of the coach, and jogged back the final couple hundred yards. Often, two-hundred yards was a challenge after a couple of donuts and a cola, so we probably looked winded. He glanced at his watch and said, "Good job boys, tomorrow I want you to shave a minute or two off".

We hit the showers and headed home. We were able to successfully shave off the time he requested the next day by eating a little faster. On non-donut days, we just walked and watched the clock or sat on a bench and talked. We felt like geniuses and this was definitely the most enjoyable experience I had at the time in organized athletics. We didn't brag about our plan, due to the fear of getting caught, but privately, we were so proud we almost burst.

The afternoon of the first track meet, we got to strut around in our purple and gold track suits all day at school and leave class a couple of hours early. This gig kept getting better every day! We were middle school jocks. As we filed into the stadium, I realized we hadn't completely thought our plan through. I was pretty doggone sure I couldn't run a half-mile. That's a fair distance, and I'd gained a bit of donut weight. I started to panic. I couldn't get a deep breath and I wasn't even running yet.

Fortunately, we were both exceptional problem solvers. We noticed that before each event, the announcer would announce a first, second, and final call. We decided that we would find a place to hide upon the first call. This became the most exciting part of the track meet for us. It also allowed us to feast on candy from the stadium snack bar without worrying about being too stuffed to run later. We discovered some awesome hiding spots. I still can remember every nook and cranny of that old stadium at Troy Field. We could hear the coach yelling, "Morse, McElroy, where are you?", with increasing urgency every few minutes, but we stayed hunkered down.

After the race, we feigned deep disappointment and apologized to the coach. "Shoot. I've been working so hard, coach. I can't believe I missed that race!"

This plan was perfect for the first couple of meets. Track was a short season and we only had one meet to go. I was about to get my first school letter without breaking a sweat! Unfortunately, the coach was growing increasingly agitated. Even he was smart enough to figure out we were missing the event on purpose. He believed we had a good chance to win, based on our improving times every week in practice. We were instructed not to leave his side at any time during the final meet. Even when we danced in place claiming to have to urinate urgently, he wouldn't relent.

As we lined up for the race, I had a sinking feeling in my gut. I had never run a half-mile before. I felt like I was lining up for the Boston Marathon. When the gun fired, I took off at a reasonably good pace, figuring I could worry about slowing down later. Halfway through the first of the two laps, I was in third place. My mind started racing. What the heck! I had never scored a single point in my entire sporting career and points were awarded for the first three finishers. I could actually score a point today. Also, maybe we were on to something and would be able to market the donut training regimen in the future. We could travel the country teaching people how to do it and coach the US Olympic team!

The adrenaline kicked in, and I believed that I was going to win this race. Third place, my ass, I was going for first. We finished the first lap and I was feeling exuberant. This was the first, and only, runners high I ever experienced in my life. About halfway through the second lap my legs started cramping up. I began to think I was going to puke and was so dizzy that I thought I might fall. I determined to fight through the pain for the points though. I wasn't going to let anything stop me now.

Suddenly a pack of five or six runners zoomed by me. I reached deep inside to keep up with them, but they kept moving further and further ahead. I cramped up so badly that I needed to walk off the course and lay down, feigning a serious injury, and didn't get to finish. That was the final minute of my track career. In fact, I didn't turn out for any sports my final year of junior high.

The skull

What's the deal with nicknames today? (Having always wanted to be a standup comedian, I loved starting with that line!) The nicknames when I was in school were way cooler than nicknames today. Most elementary kids now don't even seem to have a nickname. When I asked kids at school what their nickname was, they looked at me like they didn't know what I was talking about. When they did have nicknames, they were simple and nondescriptive like "SMo" (pronounced esmo), or JLo and ARod.

The only descriptive nickname I've been given since 1980 was given to me a few weeks ago by a forty-something dude from Miami who showed up at pickleball. He was hilarious and fit right in with all of us 60 and 70-somethings. He immediately started handing out nicknames. I suggested "cool old guy" for my nickname. He appraised me closely, cocking his head like a dog for about thirty seconds, and decided that he was going to go with "comic book man". What! I've never read a comic book in my life and that sounded like a nickname for a nerd. I took great umbrage, but he assured me that he was a devoted fan of comic books and that it was a cool nickname. I think he might have been trying to pull the wool over some old guy's eyes (or eye in my case), but it's better than most of the nicknames I had as a kid, so I guess I'll keep it. Besides, as George Costanza discovered on Seinfeld, you don't get to choose your own nickname.

Maybe I just haven't met enough kids or kids wait longer to give out nicknames these days. If you hang with a group of people under thirty who have impressive nicknames email me! I have no scientific evidence currently to prove that our nicknames were better! I'm going to take a firm stand on my beliefs though, as that seems to be what people do these days. Evidence schmevidence.

I had about a half dozen nicknames that stuck before I finished college, many with the theme of being skinny. I was skinny as a beanpole and my nickname started out as Skeleton. From there it morphed to Skelly and Refugee Man. I realize Refugee Man is rather insensitive given the plight of refugees, but don't blame me. I never had any say in my nicknames. If I did, I would have chosen Ocho Loco, T-bone, Flamethrower, or a cooler nickname.

After several years, my friends finally landed on Skull right as I began junior high. This name has lasted over fifty years. It was first utilized when a girl said I was so skinny that you could see the outline of my skull. After initial embarrassment while all the girls laughed and leaned in to verbally verify that you really could see my skull, I started to appreciate this moniker. It sounded kind of badass, like I was a tough guy. It sounded especially great when people called me, "The Skull" or "Skullman", while nodding their heads and passing in the hall. I felt like a righteous dude.

While skeleton themed nicknames were my norm, there were periods of time I had a non-skeletal nickname that lasted several months. My least favorite nickname was Fishhead. I got a fungus on my cheek that was in the shape of a fish. In retrospect, maybe mom should have let me miss a day or two of school, but I'm sure she believed that all these experiences made me a better person. I don't think my parents had the slightest idea what went on at school. I was thrilled when people dropped Fishhead and began calling me skull again a couple of months later.

I was called Rubberband Man for a while in college for my contortions on the intramural basketball court. I liked that one. Especially since the name came from a song by the Spinners with the same name.

Below is a list of some of my classmates' nicknames that I can remember.

- *Stick Man … Skinnier than me with a mature look, so later morphed to old man*
- *Grease Gun … car guy*
- *Bubble…* He made the mistake of wanting to go home early once. Everyone started laughing and teasing him for being like Dorothy in the Wizard of Oz, clicking his heels to go home on a bubble.
- *Mrs. Robinson …* Easy one for Ron Robinson during the Simon and Garfunkel era.
- *Tights …* All our jeans were so tight that we occasionally needed to hold on to a bench while a friend pulled and unrolled our pants when changing for PE. However, this guy made the rest of our jeans look like bell bottoms.
- *The little woman …* This would be a politically incorrect nickname in 2020, but this was the 60's, so what did a bunch of dumb kids know. Besides, I didn't give it to him, so don't blame me! He was late for a pickup football game because he was baking cookies. I wonder if he wished he would have just said he was helping his dad work on the car in the garage.
- *Milkbone …* Ate a bag of Milkbone brand dog bones in first

grade without even being dared. Morphed to Malcom and Malcom X.

- *Ber* ... Revised from Bob. Revised to Berman, Berman Tiger, Shelly Berman, and finally shortened to Shelly. He didn't appreciate that version, especially when being introduced to gals, so that was the one I used. I was a bit of a jerk at times, believe it or not.
- *Dill Pickle*... Long story. Shortened to The Dill.
- *Froakie ... Who knows?*
- *Moose* ... Big, fast, athletic star at a 3A school, yet somehow clumsy as an ox in day to day interactions. Broke Clint's collarbone playing a two-hand touch game of pickup football.
- *Taters* ... From Idaho.
- *Haystack* ... White dude with about a six-inch high blond stack of curly hair
- *Fleabag* ... No comments needed, but I guess I just made one anyway.
- *Tabby* ... Thought he was a cool cat
- Felix ... Same
- Gumby ... No idea

I could go on for several pages, but that's more than enough scientific evidence to show how superior our nicknames were.

While I'm on a rant about the good old days, the cartoons were better in our days, too. All the cartoons today seem to need to teach a moral lesson every single episode. Can't we all just waste a little time doing stupid things like laughing uproariously when an anvil falls on a coyote's head.

If you disagree and think nicknames are better today, please email your most unique nicknames. In the meantime, give all your friends a nickname before this part of our culture dies out. Anthropologists will wonder what happened in the future if we aren't careful.

I paved the way for Bill Clinton

"Hey, Skull. Where were you Friday night? We had a @#$% awesome kegger up at Smitty's farm. How come you don't come? You a chicken?", shouted George.

I squirmed in my seat. I hated these interactions. I had no interest in going to a kegger in seventh grade, even less interest in being teased for not going, and even less interest than that in being in the nerd group. I was also constantly riddled with guilt from my church. I slouched lower.

Smack. Bill came up from behind and whacked him upside the head. "Leave him alone. He's f***ing religious." This wouldn't be the last time my old friendship with Bill came in handy. He had my back several more times throughout school, even though we hadn't spent any outside of school time together since my first and last kegger in the fifth grade.

To not be quite as dorky, I never said, "I don't drink.", in junior high. Instead, I replied that I had quit smoking and drinking in third grade. I tried a few times when couple of my neighbor friends and a few of my cousins got into the smokes and drinks when their parents weren't in the house, so this was technically true. I held a drink or a cigarette a few times during these adventures. It was much cooler to be a recovering ex-drinker/smoker than someone who was afraid to try it. I held a cigarette and a beer several times in first and second grade, and like Bill Clinton, I didn't inhale. I didn't drink more than a sip or two of beer, either. When I had a beer, I mostly sat looking cool and pretending to sip it. I casually tossed the bottle in the trash as I left, hoping no one could see it was still about 99.9 percent full. When I had a cigarette, I practiced squinting my eyes, looking tough, and brought it to my lips now and again without ever inhaling. When I informed my neighborhood friends, I was quitting they teased me for a few days, but they didn't seem too invested in converting me. I'm not sure how I got off so easy, but

I used that line for several years.

If you are a third-grade kid reading this book, try this strategy yourself! Pretend to have a few smokes and drinks and then tell everyone you decided to quit! It's way cooler than saying, "I don't drink." Although, if you are in third grade and reading this book, you really need better parental supervision and something more interesting to do with your time. Go outside!

Poindexter

Junior high academia was so easy for me that I initially got 95-100 percent on every test and quiz I took. That didn't sit well with a few of my friends. Several times after a teacher handed back our work, they would grab me until someone got hold of my test. If I got an A, they would push me around a little and call me Poindexter or something. I knew enough basic math to figure out that if a test had 25 questions, and I didn't want an A or a B, I needed to miss about six questions. So, occasionally I purposely missed a few and then my classmates all congratulated me and slapped me on the back! Way to go, Skull. You got a D+! Parents in the 60's didn't really check their kids' schoolwork, so I wasn't worried about that. I also had to hide my homework because that was considered sucking up. If they saw it, they ripped it up. This didn't happen all the time, of course, but it happened often enough that I kept this strategy through junior high.

Many of the people that I've met as an adult found it surprising that this level of bullying didn't traumatize me more. I guess I just didn't know any differently. I assumed everyone's friends were about the same. Until my mid-30s, I assumed I had a typical American school experience. I was surprised when I found out that not everyone had the same type of experience.

Lately though, I'm starting to think these experiences were more traumatic than I realized at the time. I buried my emotions in every other area of my life. Maybe I buried my true feelings with the bullying, too. I've spent most of my life denying my feelings and fears.

Several of the school experiences have come in handy over the course of my life, especially when I was a principal. 1) Choose your battles. Live to fight another day. Run when ya gotta run and don't feel guilty about it. 2) Hold tightly to your core values, even when it requires taking an emotional (or physical!) beating. 3) When you can't control or fix a situation, at least defend those with less power than you. 4) Forgive yourself for past choices, just as you would forgive others. Most of us are doing the best we can at any given time.

Over the thirty years that I served as an administrator I interviewed well over 300 teacher candidates and only a handful had poor school experiences. Candidates typically loved school and couldn't wait to become teachers. I was the opposite. I went into education because I hated school and thought I could make a difference. I was always looking to hire someone with a similar experience, but most people who hated school had little interest in becoming a teacher. When I found one though, they were often a hidden gem.

HIGH SCHOOL
DAZE ... 1971-74

Can you finally put me in now, coach?
After not playing sports my final year of junior high, my friends talked me into trying out for basketball my sophomore year of high school. I made the team and had a blast. The coach was a decent human being, and I got to play the last couple of minutes in about half the games. I even almost made a basket once or twice. Yippee. The practices were enjoyable, too, as I got to scrimmage with my friends for an hour or more a day. Thanks, coach! This experience inspired me to turn out for the JV basketball team my junior year.

The JV team turned out to be my least favorite team sport experience. That might be
hard to believe given how poor my previous experiences were. The coach was also our PE teacher when I was a sophomore. For PE, he generally sat on the bleachers and drank coffee while a few senior TAs tormented us. If we couldn't do enough burpees, they would give us Indian burns on our arms or call us names while he watched impassively. (Native American burns? Not sure what to call these, but back in the day, they were called Indian burns and they hurt.) I'm assuming he knew my name since we only had eleven players, but he never spoke it. I didn't mind not playing in the games, as I was used to that, but the one time he put me in a game was with seven seconds left and about 1500 people in the gym waiting for the varsity game. I should have refused to go in, but I'd been waiting so long to play that I prob-

ably leaped excitedly to my feet like this was the happiest day of my life. Seven seconds? My teammates were all clapping for me on the bench. Our opponents had the ball, but I was hoping I would steal it and make a full court shot or something. Alas, I didn't. The seven seconds passed before I had time to even chase after the guy I was allegedly defending. In hindsight, I think he waited until seven seconds purposely. We had about a 30-point lead before we started the fourth quarter. He likely could have chanced it and put me in a little earlier.

About midway through the season, he stopped letting me scrimmage in practice. Now I got to sit on the bench even in practice for an hour or two every day, but still got to do all the suicide drills until I about puked. I decided to be a man and talk to him. I hoped he would recognize me when I knocked on his office door. I got about halfway through my request to get to play in practice, even if I couldn't play in games, when he interrupted to say, "Turn in your gear." I reiterated that I didn't want to quit, but that I hoped to be allowed to participate in practice. He continued to glare at me without saying another word. After an uncomfortable 60-90 seconds, I turned in my gear.

I have my father to thank for seeing my lack of success in team sports and signing me up for a park and rec tennis class at the local court. The class gave me enough confidence to try out for tennis my sophomore year. My neighbor's mom, the one who ferried me around in elementary school and "taught" me to swim, was the tennis coach and I played all three years of high school. I had a lot of fun, coached tennis at Kiona-Benton City High School, and I still play tennis regularly.

I won player of the week at the end of my senior year. Unfortunately, the weather was perfect the day the coaches announced the award, and I skipped school to go snow skiing. Some turncoat ratted me out and the coaches wouldn't give me the award. Not getting the only award I was likely to ever get in my life seemed like the perfect way to end my formal K-12 sports career.

While my K-12 sports experiences were dismal, I have been able to use these experiences to become a better coach and human being. They led me to be an educator and coach who made sure to give every kid a chance. I listened respectfully to kids and cared about them. Furthermore, I made doggone certain everyone played and felt respected when I was a coach or teacher.

As Lori Deschene says, *"Be the person who breaks the cycle. If you were judged, choose understanding. If you were rejected, choose acceptance. If you were shamed, choose compassion. Be the person you needed when you were hurting, not the person who hurt you. Vow to be better than what broke you – to heal instead of becoming bitter so you can act from your heart, not your pain."*

Girlz in the Hood

Such a cool guy

I need to inform you that I am writing this next section. under extreme duress. I had no interest in writing about why I never seemed to have a girlfriend in my teens, but Dana kept pestering me. I've always had tons of friends who were female but seemed to find myself stuck in the friend-zone every time I liked a girl as more than a pal. It's always been easy for me to be friends with females. To this day, I generally prefer chatting with women over men. Women are more interesting and have broader conversational topics than, "Did you see that Seahawks game last Sunday?".

When I did have a crush on someone, I was afraid that they

wouldn't like me back, so I never asked to be more than friends. One time, a southern gal in college kept telling me to borrow a car for my birthday because she had a big surprise for me. She spoke in a southern drawl and had a sassy attitude. I thought she was awesome. We walked and talked for about an hour every day after dinner and she took my arm and poured out her little southern heart to me.

I borrowed a car from a buddy and looked forward to my birthday all week. As we glided through the gates of the campus, she proceeded to boss me around all night telling me where to take her to do a bunch of shopping and errands. When I tried to hold her hand, she was shocked. Didn't I know that I was her best friend in the whole college? She would never ruin such a great relationship by getting involved in a boyfriend type relationship. I guess the big surprise was that I got to drive Ms. Daisy all around town for an evening. After numerous experiences like this, I lost even more confidence and was terrified to ask a girl to be more than friends.

After I was deeply enmeshed in the fear zone, there were several times that I found out months later that a girl I had a crush on was really interested in me, as well. Of course, by then they had another boyfriend and I was much too gentlemanly to butt in. Aye caramba. I couldn't win.

For the last 40+ years, I assumed that the reason I had so many close female companions was because I was funny and a nice guy. That was probably true. I am nice and certainly you realize how hilarious I am by this part of my book!

I ascertained the reasons why they weren't interested in being more than pals was…
1) I was skinny as a toothpick.
2) I wore crummy clothes and didn't try to dress nicely because I was a wannabe hippie.
3) My dad cut my hair using a bowl and I looked like Jim Carrey

in "Dumb and Dumber". I also had a humungous cowlick that I was teased about. After being teased mercilessly a few times for using gel, I decided pretending I didn't care was a better strategy.

4) I was kind of a dork. My cool factor was hovering right around zero, no matter how casually I leaned against my locker.

5) I had acne.

6) I was a goofball and "too silly" for a serious relationship, which seemed extremely crucial to these girls, even back in the fifth grade! No one told me that. Funny and nice were just grand for a friend, but when it came to boyfriends, girls seemed to want the bad guy with the fancy car, the James Dean stare, and the cool haircut and clothes.

After years of thinking I had it all figured out, Dana made me rethink my theory last week. He reminded me that plenty of dorky, skinny, acne covered guys had girlfriends all the time. So, I humbly replied, "Ok, wise Zen master. Please enlighten me on this topic.", while muttering in my head what a jackass and know-it-all he was.

Dana's grand theory was that I put off an "I couldn't care less" vibe and would never put myself out there. I acted too cool to give a rat's ass. I didn't comb my hair or wear decent clothes. My attitude declared to the world, "I'm right here, ladies, but you have to do all the work. I am much too cool to spend any effort trying to impress you. You want a piece of this, come get it." Unfortunately, there wasn't a long line interested in trying to break that door down.

When Dana told me this, I initially balked, but after thinking through it for a day or two, I knew he had nailed it. I also realized that this same attitude has been a problem in almost every area of my life for over 50 years. So, I reluctantly decided to add these thoughts to my book.

Laketa told me one time that I never made her feel like I needed her, or anyone really. It broke my heart to realize I was still putting off those vibes and not opening myself up in my mid-40s. I began working harder at letting my guard down and letting her see I needed her. I asked her yesterday if she still felt that way and she said, "No, not anymore.", so I must be making some progress.

Growing up, I suspected I was the dumbest/ugliest/dorkiest kid anyone had ever met or heard of. A few well-placed bullies were happy to confirm my suspicions. I compensated by making sure everyone knew that I didn't care, because I was so cool that I could pull it off. Inwardly, I was afraid that if I gave a 100 percent effort at something and still failed, it would crush me. If I tried as hard as I could, and still was the worst player on the team, didn't have a girlfriend, wasn't in the popular group, etc., I wasn't certain I could live with that. I was saving my effort for a must win situation. This fear of failure limited me severely in every area of my life and still does. I seldom let anyone know I was trying or gave an effort. There were a few times though, where I let my guard down and put it all out there.

The first time I called "all-in" on the poker game of life was when I met Laketa. She was a couple of years older and gorgeous. For the record, she is still a couple of years older! And, still beautiful. We were good friends for years, as I was scared to consider asking her to be more than a friend. I finally decided that I was willing to take a risk and live with the failure, so I dove in the ocean headfirst, just hoping I could figure out how to swim.

The second time I went all-in was with my kids. It was almost scary how much I loved them, and I wasn't afraid to show it. The saying that having a child is like living with your heart on the outside of your chest was true for me.

The third time I gave the full 100 percent and didn't care if I failed or looked like a fool was when I became a principal. I was passionate about the opportunity to make a difference through this role. I wanted to change the world, or at least a small piece of it.

Every decade that I've survived on this spinning orb, I've become a bit less fearful and more willing to put myself out there. I've failed enough by now to know it won't kill me and might even help me grow. I hope this trend continues if I'm still around. As I've shared this story with people, I'm finding I was not alone. Even people who exude tremendous confidence had the same inner fears holding them back, especially when it came to dating in high school. My "too cool, I'm not going to try" attitude still comes out at times, but I'm getting better at being vulnerable and honest.

Having so many female "just friends" helped me a lot in a field where about ninety percent of the elementary teachers were female. I had a blast working in elementary schools and continued to have many close female friends.

If you have something funny to say, tell the whole class
This was the best advice I ever got from a teacher, and I followed it with great enthusiasm. It was difficult to break this habit, as it was immediately rewarded with an endorphin shot due to the uproarious laughter of my classmates. I always figured, "Hey, you told me to do it."

In my administrative career, I was able to use this numerous times to make the meetings more enjoyable for almost everyone. Unfortunately, it was usually the facilitator or my boss who was the least impressed. This wasn't helping my career, so I tried to figure out when to hold 'em my last five or six years of work. Better late than never!

I learned to let my voice ring out fearlessly and often at an early age. Thank you for your encouragement, teachers.

Never Change, Man

Dana, Joni, Laketa, and I parked the car in the Marriot parking lot and started towards the door. We were heading to our 20-year high school reunion. We were a little early and were one of the first groups to arrive. As I entered, the greeter asked what I was up to now. When I informed him that I was a school principal, he started laughing and said, "You're f***ing hilarious. You haven't changed a bit. Never change, man. Never change." I attempted to convince him that I really was a principal, but he kept laughing harder and harder. "Stop man, you're killing me." I gave up and entered the venue.

For the next hour or two, in his role as official greeter, he told EVERY single person that entered the venue that I hadn't changed a bit and was telling everyone that I was a school principal. Every conversation I had that evening opened with the person telling me that they had heard I was telling everyone I was a principal and I was still f***ing hilarious. Aye, aye, aye. To be honest, I didn't really enjoy the reunion. I wanted a genuine chance to catch up with people and ended up unable to even have a conversation. Every attempt turned out like the one I described with the greeter. Old friends and acquaintances just slapped me on the back and told me how funny I was while admonishing me to "Never change man.".

In my 20s and 30s, I was often disappointed when I went back to Auburn to visit family and old friends, because I reverted to the way everyone expected me to act when I was in high school. I became the hilarious guy again for the weekend and didn't really connect meaningfully with family and friends. On the drive back home, I lamented to Laketa that I wished I had let people see the "growing" me, not only the old me.

I missed a lot of opportunities as a school principal and in my personal life by trying a little too hard to be funny all the time. There were times I could have been more helpful had I been a little more serious.

This quote in "Cold Tangerines" by Shauna Niequist really resonated with me. "When I am at my best, I can see and think and feel at a deep level, and when I am at my worst, I'm a tap dancing, tipsy show-off, with funny stories and hand gestures and painfully little else."

All in all, I did all right, I guess. The principal mantle gave me more credibility and people took me seriously when it was important to. Even so, I think 20 percent less goofing around would have been about the right amount. It's still not too late to become a little more serious in the right circumstances. Maybe there's hope!

Bill to the rescue one last time.
My senior year in high school, Bill saved my skin one final time. I was cutting through a hallway that my friends and I seldom used. It was just intimidating enough that it wasn't worth saving a few seconds. I was strolling through using my cool walk, practicing my James Dean stare, and feeling like I was king of the school yard.   I didn't even get halfway down the hall before a football player picked me up off the ground by my coat, slammed me up against a locker, and yelled, "Who gave you permission to be in this f**king hall?" I wasn't sure what to say as nobody had given me official permission. It was spring and I was just getting senioritis. I was getting careless. About ten seconds later, Bill came up behind him and slapped him up the side of the head. You could have heard a pin drop in the hall. Everyone was hoping for a brawl and ready to pick a side, but Bill just calmly proceeded with, "I have an announcement to make, so everybody listen the f**k up. This was my best f**king friend in the fifth grade and if anyone ever lays a hand on him, you will f**king deal with me. Any questions?"

As there were no questions, I thanked Bill, and continued on my merry way to class. I proceeded to cut through that hallway for the remainder of the year while all my goober pals went around the long way. I waited for them at the other end and greeted them daily with something to the effect of, "It's about time, losers." I never got tired of using that line and it brought me a huge grin again writing it today. As my nephews and friends will attest, I never tire of telling the same stories and jokes over and over. Even if others don't enjoy hearing them over and over, they crack me up every time.

I'm thankful that I decided to take a step or two away from my friend group in late elementary school. Knowing what I know about kids now, the odds of breaking away from a group of friends are low, and I'm not sure how I managed to form a completely different peer group. I'm grateful though. I will likely never spend much time with the old gang in this world, but if I see these guys again, I'll say, "Thanks for the good times and for saving my ass several times. I hope you are well. How are your grandkids?".

Cat's *in the cradle*

Me, Dad, Clint at NASCAR

Every time dad spoke to me in high school, I felt myself getting irritated. I felt bad about it but couldn't seem to control my reaction. Oscar Wilde penned, "Children begin by loving their parents, as they grow older, they judge them, sometimes they forgive them."

That's a perfect description of my progression with dad. Now that I know how darn hard it is to be a parent, I feel bad for being so judgmental. I didn't forgive him until I was in my 40s, but I'm thankful I reached that stage.

Dad was a good man, beloved and respected in the church and community. He worked hard his whole life and never said a harsh word to us kids. He took me hiking and did stuff with just me, even though there were five kids. He did the same for all of us. In some ways he was ahead of his time. My friends thought I had a great dad. He always greeted them and was kind and friendly.

Like most dads of his era though, he rarely showed emotion and was completely uninvolved in the day to day operations at home. He ceded that to mom. My sibs and I often felt like he wasn't "there", even though he was home a lot. Besides never once saying, "I love you", he always seemed to be invisible behind the newspaper.

My siblings and I all developed anger towards dad for not protecting us from Mom. He never intervened or got involved, even when she crossed the line. It made me think of him as weak and ineffectual. If memory serves me well, I felt like I needed to take care of my own stuff, even by the first or second grade. He lost his role as protector in my eyes and I decided I would figure it out myself.

He also didn't stand up to Mom when she berated him. When she was upset, she called him names and put him down. He sat silently and never replied. This made me lose respect for him and it was hard to like him as a teen. My friends couldn't figure out why I didn't like him. He seemed nice enough to them. He was also always sweet to Laketa and she didn't get it either. He treated her like a daughter from the time he met her until he died. I'm thankful for that.

Dad was never interested in the same things I was. He missed about 100 school and youth league sporting events in a row before he asked if I would like him to come to one of my high school basketball games. I was kind of shocked, but I knew he wasn't that interested in team sports and I hated to torture him, so I let him off the hook. Also, I never got to play, so it would be kind of embarrassing to ask him to leave work early to sit and watch me sitting on the bench for a couple of hours. He missed all of Clint's games, too, until Clint's senior year in football. Clint started getting college attention and his name in the paper, so dad attended the rest of the games. Clint wasn't that impressed, as he was already struggling with feeling like any love or attention he received was conditional, based solely on performance. Starting to attend after he was a star only deepened that feeling.

Dad occasionally asked me to help work on the car or watch the auto races with him, but I seldom accepted. I hated working with my hands, and I was only interested in the big three (football, basketball, baseball). I couldn't sit still for a 3-hour car race on tv and just wanted to play and move all the time. If I could do it again, I'd say "yes" a few times. I'm sure he was disappointed, but never pressured me or made me feel bad. Clint liked to help him more than I did, and he and Clint always seemed closer.

After Clint started making a lot of money, Dad became extremely proud of him and bragged about him all the time to the rest of us. Clint hated it, as it reinforced the message that you had to perform to be loved. We weren't huge fans of it either but enjoyed teasing Clint about it. I won the "Principal of the Year" Award sometime around the year 2000 and Laketa wanted me to call dad and tell him. She kept encouraging me to do it, so I finally called. The conversation went something like this.

Me: Hi, Dad. Just called to let you know I won an award at work.

Dad: You know Clint won a big award and had to fly to Chicago. I think the president was there. (Continues talking about the award for a few minutes.)

Me: Yeah, I heard about that. That's awesome. I'm proud of my little brother. Anyways, I was just calling to tell you about this award I won.

Dad: You know Clint's business won an award, too. (Continues to talk about this award for a couple of minutes.)

Me: Yeah, I heard about that, Dad. You sent me an article from the paper, remember? That's awesome. Anyways, it was great talking to you. I gotta go.

I wasn't mad. This was about the reaction I expected. It was kind of annoying though. I didn't even get to tell him what the award was called or what it was for.

A year or two after that, Mom and Dad were driving my Aunt Rae back to Canada. They were going to be passing through Bellingham during the school day and Aunt Rae wanted to see my school and convinced them to stop. I was excited because they had never visited me at work, and I was eager to introduce them to everyone and show them what I did for a living. Unfortunately, Aunt Rae couldn't get them to get out of the car and come in. Dad wanted to read the paper and mom was knitting. I went out and attempted to talk them into coming in, but they were content with what they were doing and not that interested in coming in.

Aunt Rae wanted to see everything and was excited and proud of me. When I introduced her to people and they said they enjoyed working with me, she just beamed and told me what a great job I was doing and how proud she was of me.

I wish I had a more emotional attachments to my parents. I think I disassociated by age seven or eight. This stunted my emotional growth and made it hard for me to emotionally connect with Laketa and others. I never cried or mourned the absence of a close parental relationship either. I just spent the first sixty years of my life in the denial phase. I didn't cry much at Dad's memorial, but I have cried many times recently. My tears now are not only for losing my dad, but for losing the opportunities we had after I became an adult to develop a closer relationship. He was a great guy. We just had so much baggage. I hope we get a second chance in the next world. I penned this poem recently.

Forgive me
Forgive me, Dad
For my years of anger and resentment
For my disdain,
My disinterest in any guidance you gave,
You were much wiser than I ever gave you credit for,

For never letting you fully into my life,
I was living in the valley of denial,
I didn't understand how challenging life would be,
Now I have enough scars and missing limbs to know,
I recognize that you, like all of us, were doing the best you could,

I am ready to let go,
Like a leaf loosening its grip and falling from a tree,
I forgive you for seeming absent behind your newspaper,
For never coming to my sporting events,
For not helping when mom had lost it and needed support,
I suppose that kind of help wasn't in the dad job description in the 50's and 60's,
For not hugging me or saying, "I love you",
No one taught you,
Your dad was long gone, never to be seen again,
By the time you were five,

Now that I have stopped denying that I was hurt,
Finally released it,

And watched it soar away like a bird in flight,
I'm starting to remember,
In bits and pieces,
The many times you showed your love,
You took me on hikes and to car races,
You somehow knew when I was struggling, even though I didn't
tell you,
And resented and scorned you for even daring to ask,
You weren't buried as deeply behind that newspaper as I
thought,
When I hated sitting through church, you let me escort you to
the bank mid-service,
just the two of us, depositing the offering,
When I never get off the bench and into the game in football and
basketball,
You signed me up for tennis lessons,
When a friend and I went on a hike without telling anyone and
got lost in the dark,
You, and the trailer club men, grabbed flashlights and spread
out,
I was terrified, racing around trying to find the right path,
When you found me, you were angry and grounded me to the
trailer,
But you never in your life hit me and I wasn't afraid that you
would,
I just ran and grabbed your legs,
glad to be found,

A few hours later you lifted the grounding and invited me back
to the campfire,
With strict instructions that I couldn't run wild, I had to sit by
you,
Another man at the fire loudly announced,
"If that were my kid, he wouldn't be able to walk and wouldn't
get out all weekend,
My dad never replied to the man, he leaned in and whispered in

my ear,
"You're *my* kid and I know you've learned a lesson. Ignore him."
I leaned into your warm shoulder,

You always had a quiet confidence in me,
Uninvolved by today's standards,
but I sensed that you would be there if I needed you,
I love you, dad. I miss you.
Steve Morse 2019

Senioritis

I strolled into first period right as the bell was ringing and headed for the couch in the corner of the class. I slipped off my jacket and lay down, preparing for my daily 90-minute nap to start the day right. It's a long story, but …

The two-period DECA class was taught by a progressive teacher who gave us an inspiring speech the first day. He said that he was going to treat us like young adults, preparing to enter the adult world. We needed to set our own goals and our grade would be determined by how well we met our goals, with a promise that he would accept whatever goal and grade we chose. He was not our boss; we were a team.

Instead of proudly stepping up to the plate like the rest of the class and accepting the responsibility of an adult, I decided to test this theory to the limits of the law. I was working at Pizza Hut several nights a week and got home about two a.m. I explained my situation to him and how sleep deprivation causes teenagers to make poor decisions. Therefore, my goal was to sleep at least ninety minutes of the two-hour class every day.

He chuckled a little, thinking I was kidding. When he saw I wasn't joking, he reasoned with me that this might not be the best goal. When he couldn't talk me out of it, he said he would let me set that goal, but that I would soon discover the folly of my ways. He predicted I would change my mind and informed me he would be willing to meet with me again when I was ready.

I came in every morning committed to my goal, fell asleep almost immediately and didn't awake until the next class poured in. I easily exceeded my goal! He looked at me in an irritated way every morning, but he was stubborn enough to stay committed to his vision of progressive education. Also, the other 39 kids rose to the occasion, so he was about 98 percent successful! That's actually pretty impressive.

The final project for the term was a state DECA competition where both DECA classes, about 80-90 proud Auburn Trojans, would represent our school in a two-day competition in Seattle. We even got to stay in a hotel. A few weeks before the competition, he woke me up to inform me that it was now time to step up to the plate, and that he hoped I wasn't too late. Although, the look on his face suggested that he sincerely hoped that I actually was too late. He could barely wait for nature to teach me the lifelong lesson that would make him look like a genius.

We each got to select one event. I chose Impromptu Speech and went back to sleep. He woke me up again to inform me that even in an impromptu speech competition, it was important to be prepared. They had already announced that the general topic was business in America. We should use that essential information to be preparing quotes, looking up data, and outlining several speeches on four or five possible prompts. It's actually harder to prepare for an impromptu speech. A well-prepared student would be poised for success.

I reassured him that I had it all under control, told him not to worry, and returned to the couch. He took it all in stride knowing I would learn my lesson the hard way.

On the day of the big competition, I began to worry that maybe I could have been a tad more prepared. My stomach started flip flopping as I awaited my summons to the podium. When my name was called, I walked shakily to the stage, afraid my voice wouldn't even work. I had really messed this one up. The somber judges gave me the topic.

On the bus ride to the competition, I had decided to lead with the line of "Business is as American as Apple Pie.", regardless of the topic. I delivered the first line flawlessly and the old guys judging the event were beaming. This gave me the confidence to rattle on for the required three minutes. I breathed a sigh of relief and left thinking," that's the end of that." I would accept my last place results and return to the couch for the final two weeks of my high school career. Whew.

At the awards banquet that night, the others waited anxiously as they announced the winners. I wasn't nervous at all. I knew there was no way my name would be called, so I could just enjoy the 5-star meal. As the ceremony droned on, only one person of the eighty or so Auburn High representatives had received a trophy. That was Dana. I was happy for him. He had prepared diligently for many weeks.

When it finally came time for the speech awards, the wind was almost physically knocked out of me when my name was called to walk to the stage to receive a trophy for third place. I glanced over at the teacher and he looked dejected. I honestly felt terrible, as I knew I didn't deserve the award and he was one of the teachers I thought was a halfway decent human being. I'm sure my classmates were annoyed as heck, too, although I always was a good storyteller on the fly, so it was a good choice for my event.

Nonetheless, my sheepish feelings didn't bother me enough at the time to stop me from dancing on my chair and prancing all the way to the bus waving it around like I had just won the Super Bowl. Be honest though, are there any 17-18-year-old kids who wouldn't do the same?

Senioritis hit me pretty early. I signed up for ridiculously slack classes senior year. After my nap during DECA, I strolled down the hall to Bachelor Living, where boys were taught to cook and sew, just in case they didn't get married. Can you imagine a man having to cook! That poor Home-Ec teacher was in tears a couple of times a month. We were throwing food and messing around the whole time. I was probably one of the best-behaved kids in that class.

Following that, I was a teacher's assistant for one period, which meant a two-hour lunch on the town now and again. Attendance didn't seem to be a major concern at our school in the early 70's, and many of my teachers didn't seem to mind when I wasn't there. I followed lunch with a study hall period where I didn't have any homework to do, as I was rarely assigned homework with this schedule. I often skipped this class because the teacher usually didn't take attendance and there were some terrifying guys in there. When I did attend, I pretended to be asleep with my head on my desk in an effort to not be targeted. To be honest, I was afraid of most of the girls in that class, too. Add in a fun German class, a couple of PE classes, and a typing class and you now know my two-semester schedule for my senior year.

It was quite a challenge to get into the typing class. A friend and I requested a transfer mid-quarter when we looked through the window and saw fifty girls and zero boys in the room. The counselor attempted to talk us out of it, as it was a class primarily for girls. A male typing? And aren't you two already taking bachelor living? He was genuinely concerned. He feared others might think something was wrong with us. We wore him down though and he reluctantly let us in. You would think that the fifty girls to two boys' ratio would improve our odds of landing a girlfriend, but it didn't seem to help much.

The school let me leave four or five weeks early to go out and log to save money for college. I think they were glad to get as many of the knuckleheads out as early as possible. Mom picked up what little homework I might have, and I did it in about an hour every Saturday and walked through the line in June.

I always crack up when I hear people griping about how lazy kids are these days. Some of us seemed pretty lazy back in the day. Now the kids take advanced courses in trigonometry, calculus, biology, chemistry, etc. They volunteer and participate in "activities" and try to get a high GPA just hoping they can get into a college. I'm not as pessimistic about this generation as many boomers. I met some great kids in my work who want to make the world a better place.

DECISIONS, DECISIONS

Now that I had completed high school, I had to decide what to do for a career. My only interests were rock star, standup comedian, NFL star, or teacher.

Rock and roll Icon

I was shaking my head, moving my hips, and singing at the top of my lungs. Our three-person band was in perfect harmony singing "Happy Together" by the Turtles in the stairwell of Rick's house. As band founder, I encouraged the team following every run. We were giddy and would have been high fiving and dapping, but neither of those celebrations had been invented yet. Suddenly the door burst open and Rick's mom poked her head into the alcove.

"Where did you learn that song and why are you singing the devil's music in *my* house. This will not continue".

We calmly explained that this song wasn't about drugs or sex. It had a pleasing, almost church-like harmony, and a positive message of spreading happiness. Like a bad judge, she didn't seem to be focusing on our response and was unable to see our coherent reasoning. She told her two boys that under no circumstances would they be joining a rock band, and she let me know that she would be getting on the phone to my mother immediately. What sounded like harmless lyrics were probably a satanic code for something. This was my second unsuccessful attempt to start a start a rock band and now, at only twelve years of age, that was the end of my rock music career.

It's a long story, but with another break or two at the right time, I might be in the Rock and Roll Hall of Fame today. I'll start at the beginning.

My first bad break came when I got kicked out of the fourth-grade school orchestra. The music teacher had no patience for musicians who were also training to be standup comedians. I wanted to keep both options on the table at that point in my life. I was only ten years old. We also faced artistic differences about the song "Monkey in a Cage". My artistic opinion was that making monkey noises and howling during the winter concert would add to the overall impact of the song. I couldn't help but notice that many of the fathers and siblings in the audience agreed wholeheartedly with me. It was a great addition to an otherwise boring concert. She apparently didn't care about audience enjoyment. Maybe she was burned out.

Our artistic differences and her unwillingness to allow me to make a dull class and concert series more interesting led her to terminate my contract in January with the fourth-grade orchestra. When I had similar artistic differences with the lady giving me piano lessons, I decided to go it alone in fifth grade, much like many of my rock heroes. I didn't need a bunch of dumb adults teaching me how to make music. I was already beyond anything they could offer.

I pleaded with my parents for a drum set. They foolishly said "yes", in a decision that I am convinced haunted them for the rest of their lives. I can picture them startling awake from a nightmare about drum noise well into their twilight years. At the time, they were probably desperate for anything that would get me to stop talking for a couple of minutes.

I quickly recruited a friend who had access to his dad's guitar, another with a tambourine, and three neighbor girls to be the backup singers and dancers. I wasn't going to add the horns and orchestra until after my first album. The first practice session was going brilliantly until we took a break to decide on a name for the band. My first choice was "Steve and the Gorillas". I was set on a primate name and didn't want to copy my favorite group, *The Monkees.* (You might notice a primate theme throughout this book. Primates have caused many of my problems over the years. I had detention for a week in fifth grade for not putting away my *Barrel of Monkeys set* during math, and I found myself in hot water again at a principal meeting forty years later for shouting "Stop treating us like trained monkeys" to the superintendent.)

I digress. We brainstormed several suggestions, but the debate became heated when one of the backup dancers questioned why every band name had to start with "Steve and the ...". While I understood there would be compromises in keeping a band going, this was a nonstarter for me. I always wanted my name in lights! Besides, back up dancers were a dime a dozen, but where would she ever find a drummer with my skillset or anyone with my band leadership skills. Ultimately, after about two more minutes of intense debate, in a decision that hurt their futures forever, all three dancers aligned and refused to compromise. They stormed out of the house angrily, slamming the door behind them. The lead guitar player followed them out the door, as he had a crush on one of the dancers. I had no choice other than to disband "Steve and the Gorillas", after less than an hour. If it had been the age of twitter, I would have tweeted it out to tens of thousands of fans. Instead, I just told my mom and went outside to play basketball.

This setback would not thwart my career aspirations though. At a sleepover at Rick's house, *I'm a Believer* came on the radio. Hearing my favorite group, "The Monkees", talk about belief inspired me to cautiously express my dream to Rick. Rick jumped enthusiastically on board. He was a year older, and as a sixth-grade student, I knew he would bring some maturity to the group. He would help hold the band together during challenging times. If only he had been with the band a week earlier, "Steve and the Gorillas", might be a household name.

Unfortunately, his 9th grade brother overheard us talking about starting a band and demanded to be a member. We weren't too thrilled about this, as he was quite a bully and would likely put a damper on our creative flow. However, we couldn't say "no", as he regularly put us in headlocks and tortured us. I experienced both the Chinese Water Torture and Indian Head Burn from him multiple times over the years. Both tortures were quite popular with school children in the 60's but have kind of politically incorrect names by today's standards. I am beyond thrilled that no one had heard of waterboarding back then. Just thinking about that makes my stomach churn as I'm typing this sentence. That would have been miserable.

That was my second band and the one that was disbanded when Rick's mom burst in to end our careers. I suppose it turned out just as well to throw in the towel early, as I couldn't carry a tune, play an instrument, find the beat, or dance. This never did change. As an adult, people grinned when they heard me singing in church and snickered watching me dance when we went out. I took swing dance lessons several years back under the premise of "certainly it is a skill anyone can learn". After six weeks, I was the only one in the class still unable to find and keep a beat. Following extensive genetic testing, I discovered that I had inherited "White Man Rhythm Syndrome" directly from my Irish father. My dream of becoming the first successful white rapper ended up going to Eminem.

However, I did take Joel to see Eminem in "8-Mile" when he was thirteen. This was one of many parenting decisions that Laketa and I didn't see completely eye to eye on, but she sent us on our way. She had learned to choose her battles wisely and it didn't end up messing him up too badly.

So, I was now down to three career choices.

Standup Comedian
My older sisters, Cheryl, and Karen were at least partially to blame for this interest. They were about ten years older than me and gave me a lot of attention. They were exceedingly kind. They laughed at all my homemade jokes and encouraged me to tell another one starting when I was four or five years old.

Given that storytelling and making people laugh were, and still are my favorite activities, this was an easy choice. I also always seem to want to be the center of attention. I'm getting a bit better at not having to have all the attention, in my humble opinion, but you might get an argument from people who worked with me. I don't suppose I'll ever completely lose that personality trait (or flaw?).

I entertained my family and classmates with jokes from the minute I woke up until I finally fell asleep at night, usually after multiple warnings of a spanking. I got many of my jokes from the library at school, but also made up my own. In the fourth grade, I talked the principal into letting me lead a school assembly. I was crouched down inside a rolling garbage can with a microphone doing stand-up (or crouch down) comedy. The stated objective of this performance was a powerful anti-littering message. I told the principal that this was a message every student needed to hear! I was on the forefront of the environmental movement. If we had social media in the 60's, I may have been an early version of Greta Thunberg. The principal let me have my day in the sun either because she was exhausted telling me no, or she assumed that I would get some of my smart-alecky ways out of my system in a more positive manner. Unfortunately, it didn't work out that way. The school-wide attention broadened my loyal base of fans and encouraged me to double down on my aspirations to pursue standup comedy.

I was always more than willing to take detention and swats to keep my standup comedy dream alive. In junior high, I was even willing to take swats from a PE teacher, who was an ex-Marine, for the positive social attention. Many of my peers drew the line at the math teachers. His arms were enormous.

While the pain was excruciating, it was worth it. You have to be willing to sacrifice to meet your goals. I would never make it in comedy if I couldn't take a few minutes of pain to get the attention and high-fives all day long. I could be a hero for the low price of about three minutes of pain, and it was only searing pain for the first thirty seconds or so.

This guy definitely had a few unresolved childhood issues. He would purposely set us up by pretending that he needed to leave the gym for a minute, in the hope that one of us would break the arbitrary and stupid rule he invented on any given day. One chilly winter morning, we were standing on the sideline of the gym in our PE outfits shivering our skinny little butts off. He announced he had an important phone call and informed us that if anyone moved off the line, talked or jumped on the trampoline while he was gone, it would result in two consecutive swats. There were enough little ratfinks around that people usually didn't break the rules behind his back. Those kids never would have made it in the mafia.

The second the gym door closed, kids started leaning forward (while keeping their toes firmly implanted on the line) and motioning for me to get on the trampoline. I used my astounding thirteen-year-old willpower to resist for about twenty seconds before heading directly for the trampoline. I couldn't ponder my decision long, as he might come back any time. I remember the exuberance of soaring through the air feeling like the king of the world. Ah, those were the good old days. I don't have much opportunity for that kind of acclaim anymore. I had the admiration of about fifty middle school boys for the time being and would be treated like a rock idol for the rest of the day. I hoped for a long fake phone call.

Suddenly, the door to the gym swung open and my cocaine-like high turned into a punch in the gut. At least what I think cocaine would feel like. I decided not to use cocaine, meth, or heroin as an elementary school principal. It might have helped on quite a few days though!

When Roosevelt Elementary became an arts focus school, I auditioned for and literally begged for the lead part before each of the several staff performances every year. The director, Terri McKee, never gave me the lead part, even under the threat of a failing teacher evaluation. However, she was kind enough to write a part in for me where I got lots of laughs and could do a Chevy Chase type scene where I tripped and fell. A parent asked if I would get L & I for pretending to fall off a ladder onto a mat. "Of course!", I replied. "It's part of the job!" Unfortunately, that comment and several similar parent phone calls to the superintendent impacted my ability to get promoted. Oh well, I was getting some much-needed attention!

I worried about the lack of attention post-retirement, but Cruz finds me hilarious, so I'm set! Standup comedian remained on my list, but I could practice no matter which college I selected.

NFL star

The NFL seemed unreasonable at this point. I couldn't even make my school teams. I didn't even seriously consider a side-walk Kool-Aid franchise dream. As a kid, I found it too boring and couldn't sit still that long. I kept leaving my post and the neighbor kids drank all my Kool-Aid. Also, there is not near the market for Kool-Aid as there was in the 60's, because parents are getting so doggone health conscious. I needed to just pick somewhere and go.

As it turned out, I discovered another way to make a living and still satisfy my constant need for attention. I got to sing, dance, and perform to 600 kids at a time at weekly assemblies! I may not have performed in a stadium with thousands of screaming fans, but I performed for kids who I loved and that loved me. And now I'm writing a book. Writing a book is a little bit like the baseball players playing in an empty stadium during Covid-19, but I'm enjoying it. Thanks for reading along, even if I can't hear you cheering. Send me an email instead!

ANIMAL HOUSE
... 1975-1979

Actually, it was more like "Little House on the Prairie", as I attended three different Christian colleges and the first one was in Montana. If I decide to audit university classes for free as a senior citizen, I'll redo my experience and streak across campus like Will Ferrell in the movie, "Old School."

Paul Bunyan

It was 9:30 in the morning on a hill just outside of Mineral, Washington. I was standing on a steep hillside and every muscle in my body was screaming out in pain. I had only been working for two hours my first day as a choker setter for the St. Regis Logging Company. You might wonder how a fit college guy could be so tired in only two hours. For the record, my supervisor and teammates decided not to tell this "stupid @#$% college kid" how to set a choker properly and I was literally laying on my back with my cleats dug into the log pulling with all my might each time I set a choker. My biceps and legs were trembling, and we still had six hours to go. I later figured out that if you followed the curve of the bell it was about a hundred times easier.

Learning about a bell curve came in handy in teacher college, also! A great tool to label students and make sure that some won't succeed.

Suddenly, we all heard a crashing sound up the hill a bit. The slinger (the lead for the three chokermen) tripled his swearing immediately. Prior to hearing this, I wasn't sure that was even possible. You had to listen intently to figure out what he was telling you to do even in nonemergency situations. I cocked my ear like a dog when he started in, trying to decipher the meaning, "Hey, @#$% !@#$ stupid college %$& $&&$, take the $&%& #&#& to the $%$ $#$%&, and then get your $%*#& #& $&$ over to the $%($*#& and #$$&#^#& the $#*#*#**#." I just hoped I did whatever I was asked to do. I felt like I should get a certificate of merit for learning a second language by the end of the summer, but the company didn't find my request that humorous.

"What did you say?", I shouted in fear.

We were all alarmed by the greater urgency in his voice and the crashing noises up the hill. He picked me up and tossed me behind a stump and bear hugged me from behind, pushing me into the stump. I began fervently praying that this was not some kind of initiation ceremony. A few seconds later we all saw a giant log go rolling past us about fifty feet to the right. This was terrifying. I had only worked in the woods a couple of hours and was physically exhausted, had almost been killed, and had experienced a "Deliverance" style orientation with a stump and my boss. I wasn't sure I would make it until lunch time.

The slinger turned me loose and explained that you never run from a root wad or log because they can hop fifty yards left, then fifty yards right, etc. Almost like our current political system. They don't careen straight down a hill. Instead, you take cover behind the biggest stump you can find so it will hit the stump and go over your head. He had possibly saved my life, depending which way that log hopped.

"Could you repeat that? ARE YOU KIDDING ME?", I thought in my head. This job was sounding worse by the minute. Maybe I should walk back to camp right now and find a different way to pay for college.

The slinger also seemed to have a crush on me. We had a crew of three chokermen. There were no chokerwomen in 1974 in our company. I bet there are now! We would each set a choker and a machine would pull the logs up the hill, as we watched hoping they would not break loose and come rolling down the hill in an attempt to kill us. (Sorry for not knowing all the technical names. Things will mostly just be referred to as machines, except for when I occasionally know a mechanical name. I'm more of a big picture person.)

Once the logs were at the top, we had a three- or four-minute break before another machine took the logs and stuck them on a truck. (I know the term for truck!) Then the original machine sent the chokers down on a pulley for us to set again. A couple of times a day, during this brief break, he asked me if I wanted to wrestle.

I said, "No thanks", about forty times over the course of the summer. All twenty to thirty times that I said, "No thanks.", he laughed and threw me on my back. I usually landed on a stick or log or stone, as interestingly enough, there were no wrestling mats on the forest floor. He then flipped me over to my stomach, got on my back and started twisting my arms and practicing the moves he was so great at in high school while regaling the other chokermen with his high school feats of glory. Dana never told him to lay off, partially in fear of being the next target and partially because he thought it was hilarious. Cincinnati Fred never said anything either. Apparently, they didn't have a rigorous sexual harassment training for supervisors in the logging business in 1974.

In fact, they didn't seem to have any training for anyone that worked for this company. To get hired, I had to go out and buy all my gear. Gear included cool logging suspenders and wide jeans cut about capri length below the knee so I wouldn't trip, awesome boots with long metal spikes so I could walk across logs suspended over other logs, and a really funky steel helmet like the guys wore in the movies when they walked on steel girders 100 stories above New York in the old days. I looked like a tough dude!

Once I looked like a logger, I stood on the side of a gravel road, where Dana's brother told me to stand, at 4:30 AM while letting crew buses, like the short buses at school and called crummies, roar by and kick up dust at me in the hopes one would be short a guy that day and would stop and pick me up. After several days, a crummy stopped, I boarded and was officially hired! (This was not nearly as rigorous as the hiring process we used for teachers.)

After I lived through the day, they dropped me off at a little shack to fill out all the forms for social security and the address to send my check to if I got killed tomorrow. I was now hired and assigned a crew! All my training was on the job training, which was basically my boss and the other guys laughing at me while I did everything wrong until I finally started doing some stuff right.

Dana helped me get this job through his brother who worked there. We also got dinner every night and a place to park our trailer at his house in exchange for helping with the haying on his small farm for a few days in August. Wow. Fantastic deal. We were ripping that guy off! (Unfortunately, he had lights in his barn, and we hayed until midnight when the hay came in and then got up at 3:40 to catch the bus by 4:30 the next morning. Didn't seem like that great a deal that week.)

This was my first summer job during my college years. We were going to be rough and tumble loggers. I thought of myself as a real "man's, man" for a few months. For some reason though, no one has ever used that phrase as a description of me in the other 64 years of my life. If you know me personally, please describe me that way in a group setting at some point in the future. On second thought, don't, that phrase is kind of offensive now days and I'm really working on being a more balanced individual.

After a few weeks I was informed that I was now experienced enough to carry the dynamite around all day. The dynamite was used to blow a hole under the logs that fell on the ground and buried themselves a foot or two into the ground. We didn't light a fuse like in the cartoons. Instead, it was some kind of an electric spark that set it off from a remote carried by the slinger. For much of the day, our slinger pretended he was going to push the button and yelled, "Boom". I didn't really enjoy this little game that much.

At the end of the day I didn't know where to store the dynamite overnight. I didn't want it to get wet. I had learned in the first three weeks to never ever ask a question, no matter what. Asking questions led to a great deal of verbal abuse and were never answered anyways. So, I used my best judgment and tucked it under the glove box area in the front of the crew bus. About ten minutes into the ride back to camp, the driver let out a torrent of swear words and stopped the bus.

"Who in the @#$% @#$% @#$% left the @#$% @#$% @#$% dynamite @#$% by the @#$% @#$% @#$% electrical box in the @#$% @#$% crummy. We could all have been @#$% @#$% killed." I sheepishly raised my hand and that was the end of my promotion to dynamite boy. They assigned Cincinnati Fred to lug it around all day.

The only other noteworthy memories of that summer were Dana deciding that boxing would be a good way to stay in shape and meeting "Killer".

Gary had a couple of pair of boxing gloves lying around and Dana decided that climbing mountains and wrestling chokers for eight hours a day wasn't enough exercise for us two muscle-men. His solution was that we should spar a bit every evening. I wasn't too excited about his grand plan, as he weighed about thirty pounds more than my skinny ass and was probably twice as strong. A logger never backs down though, so I agreed.

I was getting pummeled around mercilessly for about five of the longest minutes of my life when Dana decided that was the end of the first round. He seemed to make all of our decisions. As I walked to my corner to rest, I was hoping he wasn't planning a fifteen round pro-style match every evening. I loved sports, but so far, this had been my least favorite sports experience ever. I knew I would get slaughtered if I just continued doing what I was doing, so I decided to work smarter, not harder. I decided not to throw any punches, but instead dodge and wait, let him land a few, and then bring a haymaker around when he missed and left himself open. It worked brilliantly. I clocked him a good one. I hit him hard enough that he staggered back a half-step. I felt like Sugar Ray Leonard or Muhammed Ali, a heavy underdog, scoring points with my wits. I was starting to think boxing might be kind of fun after all!

Dana didn't quite see it that way. He told me years later that his thought was, "Are you kidding me? Here we are having a friendly little spar to get in shape and this jackass roundhouses me with all his power." He leaped up and literally beat the holy guacamole out of me for about five more minutes. We both decided we didn't really need to exercise every night after all and went back to riding motorcycles and leaping the electric fence while letting the bull chase us around the pasture.

The other interesting day was when I was assigned to sub on Killer's crew. Dana and I were usually on the same crew and my slinger liked me, maybe a little too much. In many ways, I was getting off easy and not getting the full experience. I was ok with that though and wasn't excited about leaving for the day to work for Killer. We had been hearing the legends about Killer all summer long. Almost everyone we met led with, "At least you didn't get assigned to Killer's crew.". They followed this pronouncement with a terrifying "true" story about Killer. Legend had it that he was given the name when he killed a guy in a bar fight and was acquitted for reason of self-defense. Another story had him and his brother going to an African American bar in Tacoma, freely throwing around the "N" word, punching a guy or two, and then racing for the car. The patrons of the bar were a little bit upset and several huge guys picked up the back bumper of his VW while others surrounded the car. Killer threw the car into reverse while flooring the gas pedal, cracked the window, and announced, "You fellas interested in a truce or want to just hold onto the back bumper for a while. I have over half a tank left." They selected the option of a truce, set the car down, and he pulled away to live another day. We were never completely sure which or how many of these stories were accurate, but I was scared spitless of him.

I was scared half to death the evening before my sub day. Gary gave me some advice at dinner. He told me when he first started, Killer wouldn't lay off him, so he grabbed a chain saw, started it, and started chasing Killer all around acting like he was a little bit crazy. Killer never bothered him again.

He recommended I do the same. I was about 130 pounds dripping wet and wasn't confident that I could even start a chain saw. I pictured pulling and pulling the chord while Killer laughed maniacally behind me. I nodded along with Gary, knowing I would never implement this suggestion.

When I entered the bus, Killer put his face about six inches from mine to tell me I might not survive the day and I had better watch my #$%^ @# $% @#$& back. I had the privilege of listening to him calling me and my mom horrible names all day long. (I wonder where he met mom.) He wouldn't let me drink any water until official break times and threw pebbles at my hard hat for at least half the time I was there. I was surprised he didn't get tired of it. It didn't really hurt, but it was kind of irritating. I took my hard hat off a few minutes into lunch break, under the assumption that he wouldn't hit my bare head with a pebble. That turned out to be an inaccurate assumption, so I ended up eating with my hat on. I guess he and my slinger both missed the cultural sensitivity and harassment training day. All-in-all though, the day didn't turn out all that badly and I could now claim I had worked for Killer.

In retrospect, this job helped me grow up in a hurry. I went from sleeping on a couch and sitting unobtrusively in study hall in high school to an immediately life-threatening situation that was physically exhausting. I never had a job again that seemed all that hard or dangerous. When I worked the long days and weeks as a principal, it didn't compare to the 4:30 a.m. to midnight sessions of logging and haying.

Dana and I were telling these stories in front of Dad one day and he was mortified. He told me he never would have let me work there if he knew how dangerous it was. Luckily, we seldom communicated during those years thanks to my ungrateful attitude to a guy who really was a surprisingly good dad for that era.

If we were hired today, we would have to watch a bunch of safety videos and have a couple days of training before they sent us up to possibly die. The supervisors would likely have a little more training, too. They might be in court a lot these days. I'm still here though and those were the good ol' days!

Bible college wasn't as bad as it sounds

Dana and I on the first day of Bible college

I was standing in a group of kids in the tenth-grade commiserating about how terribly boring some church event was to Dana. Dana was as big a fool as I was at the time but came up with some unexpectedly wise advice. "You can make anything fun. Your attitude is your choice." Hmm. Pretty wise for a sixteen-year-old male. From that point on, Dana and I made every school and church event an absolute blast for everyone involved, except for the leaders, of course.

Dana's uncle helped start a small Bible College in a beautiful place in central Montana. Dana and I attended for two years and even managed to make that potentially sterile environment a lot of fun. Looking back now, I can't believe I chose to go there. I'm sure most of the professors wondered what in the heck brought me to campus. We executed endless pranks, and I took every opportunity to mock what I felt were completely ridiculous rules. In my unrequested opinion, the handbook could have been written in the 1800s. I'm surprised it wasn't handed to us on a scroll. I managed to wallpaper my dorm room with pink discipline slips spelling out the initials of the school in five-foot-tall letters within a few months. My fellow students were either extremely impressed or horrified!

I made some great friends there and learned some life lessons, but the Bible school deal wasn't where I was headed, so I only stayed a couple of years. The emphasis on outward appearances, like length of hair and dress codes, was about 180 degrees the opposite of what I thought Jesus would do. The curriculum also didn't encourage questioning or thinking beyond what I had already been drilled with growing up. This served to perpetuate the fears and issues I had with church during my childhood. The experience had the potential to make me turn completely against the church, but somehow it didn't. I mostly made fun of the dogma, collected pink slips for behavior, and let it bounce off my thick skull. The experience helped me sort the things that I wanted to emulate from my experiences in church, so I survived fairly unscathed. No experience is wasted.

Realizing that I had the choice to make any and every experience fun influenced my educational career significantly. This was a huge part of my unique style and success. Even during the throes of the back to the basics, no frills movement; I never embraced the "shut up, buckle down, and quit complaining" philosophy that was prevalent. Why shouldn't kids and families enjoy school? Children should see learning as joyful and school as a great place to be.

Twenty years after this conversation, it also ended up aligning with what I would learn about only being able to control my own reactions to situations. In fact, this life choice I made at age sixteen had as much to do with my success in education as anything I learned in college. The kids, teachers, and parents always had a lot of fun in my schools.

I especially believed that the schools with higher poverty rates, discipline issues, etc., should be even MORE fun than upper-middle class schools. Our schools with the neediest kids often look like schools from the 1950's with boring kill and drill curriculum and stern old-school discipline policies.

Personally, I believed that was 180 degrees the wrong approach. Struggling schools with high need students need more field trips, art, and recess, not less. They also need to learn how to get along and work out social issues, not miss all their recess learning opportunities to complete busy work or be suspended all the time. The teachers need to have fun and be joyful in our most challenging schools, also. I had the opportunity to live this out in all my jobs, but the staff and parents at Roosevelt really embraced this and it was my favorite experience by far.

Long story short, I never buy the excuse that something is boring. It's my choice. If you ever find yourself visiting a church in Auburn, Washington, and you pick up a hymn book that has a treasure hunt where you have to turn from page 67 to page 192 to page 23, etc., until you find treasure, you can thank my friends and me! We consistently found ways to make church a little more interesting.

Stop the assembly line

Have you seen the "I Love Lucy" clip where Lucy and Ethel are on an assembly line and they get behind and start shoving chocolates into their mouths, hats, and shirts? I had a similar experience working at a bread company my second summer of college.

I stood on an assembly line, all alone, so no one else to blame, for ten hours a day while loaves of bread came at me. My job was to grab six loaves at a time off the belt by holding my arms out straight like a robot, and then turn robotically to my right and put them on a bread delivery tray. Each tray held twelve loaves. When one was full, I moved it to the full stack and started on the next one. When it was about six feet high, the guy on a forklift took it. I wanted to trade jobs with him so badly, but I was a college kid, and he looked about fifty, so I never asked.

I was shocked by how quickly they expected us to do this. I was reasonably athletic at that age and even after several days of getting to practice for ten hours at a time, it was all I could do to barely keep up. How could someone do that for their whole life? Every few hours I would get behind and bread would start falling on the cement floor. I was so relieved when the supervisor came running over the first time this happened. I reckoned he would inform me not to worry, as this happened to everyone and it would take no time at all for the two of us to catch up. What I didn't realize, was that his strategy wasn't as affirming as I had hoped. Instead of helping, he started swearing at me in a very personal way. It wasn't a generic "Shit, what's happening." It was a personal greeting more along the lines of, "You dumb @#$%. How could you be so @#$%ing slow. Stupid college @#$%. What the hell is wrong with you?"

I didn't find this all that helpful, but I must admit, I did work faster! After a few minutes of denigrating me, he shut the machine off, and I picked up all the bread on the floor. I only fell behind like that once a day or so once I had been there a week, but his strategy never really changed. I was hoping that was a first-time message and that he would have other inspirational speeches in his repertoire for the times it happened in the future, but he seemed to be a guy that liked to stick to one basic strategy, whether it was working or not.

I left that job about three weeks later when I got offered a job at the post office. After seeing a couple of people snorting coke in the restroom, I decided this probably wasn't a good long-term career option. I never did see anyone snorting coke at the post office job.

For the record, I never caught a teacher snorting coke in the restrooms at school either. Of course, about ninety percent of the teachers in the elementary schools I worked at were female, so that only means the men weren't doing it during my tenure. I can't be too sure about the women.

The best part about my summer jobs in college was they encouraged me to stay in school!

The angle man
As we left the lunchroom to return to our stations in the post

office, I surged ahead and began scoping out the best place to work. We stood in these cubicle-like deals and sorted mail into about a hundred different slots to send mail all over the good old USA. We were supposed to sort a bin of 600 letters in fifteen minutes, but I'm not sure anyone was ever quite that fast. Also, the veteran workers would intimidate us college summer temps and tell us to slow the f*** down. They sent the biggest dudes over to our section to deliver this message and it was a little scary. They complained that we were making them look bad. Of course, they also complained we were too slow and were mad that the dumb government hired a bunch of college idiots every summer in the lunchroom, so I never knew quite what speed to go. I tried to shoot for a middle speed.

The one older guy in our group of ten or twelve summer temps was in his 30's. He had long hair and a laid-back lifestyle. He picked up temp jobs until he had enough money and then chose not to work for a few months. He was an interesting guy and fit right in with our important philosophical college lunch discussions like, "Do you think the government is hiding secrets about UFOs?"

He looked over at me as I raced past him and informed me, "I'm going to start calling you the angle man."

"What's that mean?"

"You always have an angle. You never just leave the lunchroom and stroll down the stairs and take whatever seat you happen to get."

I pondered that for a while and thought, "Shove it, old man. At least I'm not in my mid-30s and still working a temp job." However, I just replied, "Interesting."

I ended up working at the post office for the next four summers I was in college. It had the potential to be boring, but we made up games and had sorting races. We played basketball with the packages on the days we got to work in the package section. I apologize sincerely if you received a broken package in 1975 from the Sea-Tac Air Mail Facility.

Over the years, I thought back to this day many times and realized that I really am kind of the "angle man". I'm always thinking of the most efficient way to do anything. Just today, I couldn't decide which way to go in the car. After significant analysis, I finally chose one. I got stuck at a red light and was kicking myself for not choosing the other route. Good grief.

While analyzing every little thing helped me be an efficient administrator, it cost me a lot in my quest to have a peaceful mind most of the time. Slowing the hamster wheel has always been a challenge for me. I would like to be different and am working on it. Walking a mile in my shoes would be boring as all get out but spending two minutes watching the hamster wheel in my mind would be fascinating!

One of my favorite stories is from the book, "The Spirituality of Imperfection", by Ernest Kurtz and Katherine Ketcham. A Zen teacher saw five of his students returning from the market on bicycles. He asked his students, "Why are you riding your bicycles?"

The first four each had an answer ranging from the practical (to buy food) to the spiritual and Zen-like. (It gives me peace. I feel one with the universe.) After each answer, the teacher commended the student wholeheartedly for their answer. The fifth student answered, "I ride my bicycle to ride my bicycle.".

The teacher sat at his feet and said, "I am your student."

That's the way I want to learn to live. I want to be content in the moment and not analyzing every little decision. I want to just ride my bike and not try to find the shortest route or analyze why I chose to ride my bike today. I'm working towards being content with whatever I am doing.

This story reminded me of some of the kids I met playing sports in Bible College. They said stuff like, "I play for God's glory." … "It helps me stay in shape and keep my body sharp to serve God.", etc. Playing sports was one thing I never overanalyzed though, and I always thought these guys were kind of overthinking it. I wasn't sure Jesus really cared if they turned out for the team. I played football in college because I liked to play sports. I got it right once, I guess.

I guess I did learn a valuable life lesson from that old hippie after all. I'll never admit it to him though. He was kind of a know it all and thought he was so much wiser than all us college kids. If I ever see him again, I'll let him know, "I now understand your advice, but at least I had a real job in my 30s, so take that."

Rip their heads off and sew 'em back on for Jesus
I was living' the dream. I found myself encircled by twenty college football players jumping up and down shouting, "Go, go, go", before we raced out onto the field to play under the lights in front of our twenty to thirty avid fans. The player/coach signaled for quiet. We were going to pray before the game.

"Our heavenly Father, hallowed be thy name. Give us the ability to show our opponents that we are not pansy ass Christians, but real men. Help us to rip their heads right off their shoulders and sew them back on for Jesus. Amen"

What the heck? Did I just hear what I thought I heard? My mind immediately thought, "Um, count me out, God. I'm not certain that I agree with this prayer. I just turned out for football for fun."

Even at 20 years old and still in my most fundamentalist evangelical Christian stage, this seemed a bit over the top to me. This coach was a little rabid in other ways, too. Before the game he grabbed my facemask with both hands and slammed our helmets together face to face while yelling, "Get psyched", into my face from about three inches away. Besides being a germophobe and hating the spittle, I wasn't a big fan of slamming my head several times into someone who outweighed me by seventy pounds. I spent most of my pregame time keeping my one eye out for him rather than stretching.

I begged the coach to be first in line and shattered the butcher paper banner as I led my team out on the field that night. It was harder to bust through in real life than it was in the hundreds of time I had performed this in my imagination. I stumbled a little but recovered and raised my arms to the roar of the twenty or so students attending.

Later in the game I intercepted a pass and almost scored my first point in a school team sport. I was racing down the sideline full speed with the goal line in sight. Because this wasn't a "real" college field, like the Washington Huskies play on, it was hard to tell how close I was to the end zone. Suddenly, "wham", I went down like a rock. The quarterback had blindsided me (literally) and swatted all 155 pounds of me down like a fly. When I got up, I was about a foot from the goal line! If the field had been lined, I could have swerved or leaped and scored my first point. I felt like Charlie Brown and Lucy pulled out the football before I could kick it for the fiftieth time.

I was thrilled to be in the starting lineup of an official college football team, even though it was a tiny college. It was the "big-time" to me. We were the Christian Heritage Hawks and played the marines from Camp Pendleton. The marines had awesome team names like "Special Weapons Attack Team #201", "Fire Team #3" and "Expeditionary Force 1".

One team I didn't want to lose to was called the "Mail Clerks from Unit 12" or something like that. I can't remember if we beat them, but we won about half our games, so I hope we won that one! I can't imagine watching my life over again prior to entering the next world and having to watch us lose to the mail clerks in slow motion. I probably let some skinny dude in thick glasses run right over the top of me while scoring a touchdown.

I was also a starter on our basketball team. We played in the second highest division for the San Diego Park and Rec League. In a city the size of San Diego, this division was extremely competitive, and we often played against ex-small college players. My best friend had averaged over 30 points a game in high school and could really shoot. I spent most of the game passing to him, so I had a lot of assists and also averaged about eight points per game myself, so I FINALLY scored an actual point in a school sport after close to 20 seasons where I didn't score even one point. (Although, I may have been able to score one in track had I not been hiding most of the season.) I called a timeout and made each of my teammates give me a personalized high five and say congratulations when I made my first basket.

This was my second experience in a small Christian college. The fact that less than 200 students attended made me a sports star. I also got the lead part in one of the school plays. I was a big man on campus. It was located in San Diego, which was a little warmer than Montana. I learned to body board and enjoyed sunshine the entire year, a nice perk for a kid from Washington. The school was new and was just finishing the accreditation process and would be accredited the following fall.

Alas, the library didn't contain enough books and they failed the accreditation process, so I transferred to George Fox University for my last two years of college. Knowing my goal was to be a public-school teacher, I figured I might as well attend an accredited school. I still miss San Diego though and every now and again around March, Laketa and I look at each other and say, "Why the hell do we still live in Washington?".

The Hippie Dome

It took three colleges in three states and an extra year, but I finally graduated from George Fox College as an accredited teacher. George Fox is a Quaker institution and an excellent college (now a university) with a great national reputation.

On my drive down, I was worried everyone would wear a hat and look like the guy on the Quaker Oats box, but apparently Quakers in the NW today are quite modern. Walking the campus looked about like walking anywhere else I'd been walking to that point. The more I learned about Quakers, the more I respected their social activism and liked a lot of their teachings about Jesus better than my childhood teachings. Some great people.

A business major and I ended up living in a big house with some of the more traditional Quaker students. They didn't wear hats or anything, but they were hardcore hippies who protested against nuclear power and against war. They made quite a bit of money fishing in the summer and only paid half their federal taxes. They sent a note saying that they would not support the fifty percent the government spent on the military. I'm not sure if they ever were prosecuted for that, but I really respected their willingness to take a stand

The business guy and I named our house the Hippie Dome and teased the hippies mercilessly. They gave it back five times as hard, due to the fact there were a lot more of them in the house. We had a lot of fun slagging back and forth. Being a PE major, I was an easy target for them. I was now ready to begin "real" life, or so I thought.

LIFE IN SMALL TOWN AMERICA ... 1980-92

Lianne and Joel

$%#& stoplights

My first teaching job was in Benton City, Washington, a small farming town on the east side of the mountains. Summer days were often in the high 90s or low 100s in Benton City. Our Honda Civic had no air-conditioning. One of the more interesting glitches of this car was that it overheated every time you idled whenever it was hot outside. I started to absolutely despise stoplights. When idling, the only way to keep it from overheating and blowing all the water right out of the top of the engine, was to crank the heat on as high as you could every time you were stopped. This would blast some of the hot air out of the engine and right into the car. If you turned the car off when stopped, it wouldn't start again. Stoplights became my greatest nemesis and I occasionally let out a few choice words when the light turned yellow, even though this was well before I embraced cussing more fully.

We were the unpaid youth group leaders for a small Baptist Church at the time. Occasionally, we fit seven (5 high school kids and Laketa and me) in a Civic designed for four. One kid sat on the console between Laketa and I and two sat in the back with two on their laps.

We were on our way for an allegedly spiritual experience at the waterslides on one of those 100-degree days. We drove the fifteen miles to Richland with the windows all the way down to a cacophony of groaning and complaining about how hot it was jammed into the Civic like clowns in a circus car. We pulled off the exit and luckily hit two or three green lights in a row, and then ... the dreaded red light came. I cranked the heat to full, watching the heat gauge intently and praying fervently that we wouldn't overheat. This was a long stoplight that included arrows, etc., and the three or four minutes we waited were filled with moaning and groaning high school kids. This could have been a great object lesson on what hell might be like, but it didn't feel like the best time for a sermon because I think I let a few choice words out. I can still hear the groaning from the back seat as I rewrite this story. It cracks me up now but didn't seem all that funny at the time.

We had some great years on the plains of Washington. We waterskied and played tennis with a couple of the nicest people we've ever met. We stayed busy coaching, teaching, and working with the junior and senior high kids at church. Laketa was the high school secretary. It was a great first place to live and living four hours from home helped us separate from our families and make our own life. We adopted Lianne our last year there.

We ended up living in towns with either no stoplights or just a couple for the first fourteen years that I worked in education. This was awesome but made me even more impatient when I did have to stop at one. My siblings and old friends from Auburn were a little surprised that Steve, the patient teacher who never lost his temper, got so angry every time he had to stop at a red light! I'm finally able to chill at lights and we have now lived three and a half years in another stoplight-free town. Life is good.

The big time is where you are at

Coach Morse of the Bears

"Sacked by Downard and Westerfield. Second and seventeen.", I spoke into the loudspeaker at the Friday night football game in Benton City, Washington. I was sitting on a scaffold about twenty feet in the air doing the announcing for the big game against Royal City. It was about thirty degrees with a fifteen mile an hour wind whipping past me up there. Even though I was bundled up, I was freezing. We had never heard of Benton City prior to getting hired, but it became our town and our school when we moved there.

I took a college class on how to be an effective coach in college where the professor reminded us often, "The big time is where you are at." That really resonated with me. Whether I was coaching at a school with 150 kids in Eastern Washington or coaching the Washington Huskies, I treated it as important and was loyal to those kids. In every small town, their team was the big time for them. As a teacher and a principal, I treated every school community as if they were the most important in the country. I gave my allegiance and loyalty to my school, my boss, and my town.

I gave my loyalty because I felt it was the right thing to do. I understood that not everyone would reciprocate and tried not to be disappointed or surprised when people didn't. I can only control myself and be the person I want to be. While it was rare that people returned loyalty and support with disloyalty, there were times when a teacher or family would completely throw me and/or the school under the bus, even though the teachers and I had bent over backwards for them. This disappointed me at first, but I realized that it's a numbers game. Our school had relationships with over 600 families a year. With that many people to serve, there would always be a few who would throw me or us under the bus, no matter how well we treated them. I attempted to depersonalize the hurt and just did my part of remaining loyal and doing my best for them.

Clint felt the same way with his company. "In growing Mosaic I've found loyalty is not rewarded quickly, and sometimes not at all. True loyalty must be earned. It's a cornerstone of how I do business, and I pay close attention to fostering and supporting it." He also recognized that it was about him. He was going to show loyalty whether it was reciprocated or not.

As a principal I never wanted blind loyalty from the kids, teachers, or parents. Suck-ups drove me nuts. I appreciated the people who told me when I was screwing up or gave me an idea about a better way to do something. Luckily, there was a teacher (or a dozen) at every school where I was the principal who made certain to inform me when they or the other teachers thought we were headed in the wrong direction. I was sensitive at first but learned to appreciate the help and appreciated that people trusted me and could be honest with me.

I believe that one of the main reasons I had any success at all, was because I encouraged people to question me and affirmed them when they did. I couldn't ask people to question me and then rip their heads off or get pouty when they did. Teachers and secretaries saved me from a plethora of problematic decisions by being honest with me. Leaders who desire blind loyalty and close themselves off to feedback leave themselves vulnerable to making blunder after blunder. Blind loyalty leads to situations where the emperor has no clothes.

I never offered blind loyalty to my supervisors either. I let them know when something was backfiring in the world beyond their offices. Many didn't appreciate it much, and I improved my delivery skills over time, but I believed it would be wrong to just sit back and chuckle behind the scenes while they set the whole district on fire. My values required informing them. I gave the information as unemotionally as possible and left the decision up to them, rather than pushing and pleading. They were the boss. Just wanted to let them know. Anyways, my team was always the home team, wherever life took us. Rah, rah, sis boom bah.

Joni (Laketa's sister), Laketa, and me

Fear Not

Laketa, and I were camping by Mt. St. Helens, a week or two before it blew up.

Laketa and I were sitting around the campfire on a star filled night, when a friend asked us what our greatest fear was. I had to think for a while before telling him that my greatest fear was boredom. He laughed because he knew me as the guy who never sat still or stopped babbling. I'm sure I would have been diagnosed with ADHD in elementary school, had I been born about fifteen years later. I drove Laketa nuts asking her what we were going to do today the minute I woke up or got home from work. I'm getting better, but Covid-19 probably has Laketa worried about me hanging around the house for any length of time.

Being bored used to almost throw me into a panic attack. I was terrified at the prospect of extended boredom. This may have been due to my inability to reflect or develop intimacy. I kept all my feelings deeply buried and tried to never think too deeply. Some of my sibs were angry and bitter towards Mom and Dad, while I chose to stay in phase one, denial, as my first and final strategy. By not thinking too much about anything, I was a pretty happy fella. My subconscious fear was ... What if I get bored and have to think about stuff? I better stay busy 24/7.

Death was never my number one fear, at least consciously. Death seems kind of inevitable. Even when I got cancer, it didn't freak me out. However, I might sing a whole different tune if someone walked up behind me now and put a gun to the back of my head. That was a rather good possibility with one of the secretaries I worked with! Until a person stares death down in a hospital bed or war zone, no one can really know how they might react. All I know, is until I was in my mid-40s, boredom remained my biggest fear. After raising two kids and being an elementary principal, boredom has gone from a paralyzing fear to my greatest hope! When I was younger, I wanted to go out every night and stay up late. Now I want to stay home most nights and just hope to be able to stay up until 10:00 p.m.

I've read that fear of snakes is number one in many surveys, and that the fear of public speaking comes up high in every era as a top fear. Personally, I absolutely love public speaking. Here is a Seinfeld quote that cracked me up.

"According to most studies, people's number one fear is public speaking. Number two is death. Death is number two. Does that seem right? That means to the average person, if you have to go to a funeral, you're better off in the casket than doing the eulogy." *Jerry Seinfeld*

I especially enjoy impromptu speaking. The worst part of public speaking for me was having to spend time preparing ahead of the event. If I didn't have to prepare, it would be the perfect assignment for me. I still have my big DECA trophy!

I never ranked my top ten fears, but I've always been afraid of snakes. As a kid, when my buddies and I went garter snake hunting, I succeeded in never catching one. Unfortunately, they felt sorry for me, so they let me hold one of their captives. I thanked them and held the snake for a minute. My heart was pounding, but my face remained calm. I knew if they found out that I was scared of snakes, they would put them all over me. Those short reptile holding sessions were horrible. One minute seemed like four hours.

During our annual reptile assembly at Roosevelt, the Reptile Man announced to the assembled parents and kids that we were now at the part of the assembly where he wrapped his boa constrictor around the principal. I politely declined every single year. A female teacher usually enthusiastically volunteered in order to show the audience what a wimp I was. "Thanks a lot." If any of my childhood friends are reading this book, I hope you have matured by now and won't chase me with a snake next time I see you. I still think it might be too early to let that secret out.

My only other recurring fear was a couple of the ladies I worked with. I jumped immediately and asked, "how high" to a few of my secretaries' and teachers' requests. Everyone I worked with will know exactly who they are! Nonetheless, I'm proud to say, I have smashed my biggest fear to smithereens. I am ready to tackle the next one, unless it is snakes, Nancy, or Vicki.

Another piece of straw for the camel's back

Laketa and I were sitting in an uncomfortable "1600's style" pew in our small Baptist Church in Benton City. We had just returned from a month-long vacation and it was good to see our old friends. We also missed the kids. We had grown close to many of the kids after volunteering to lead the youth group for the past several years. The pastor had an important announcement that was great news for our youth.

Our ears perked up. The youth group had grown from fewer than five kids to over thirty for special events. We were proud of our work and loved the kids. Maybe someone had donated a van or given money to send our group on a trip!

The pastor leaned into the microphone. "I am pleased to announce that I have recruited new youth group leaders. Jim and Julie have agreed to take on this important job. Let's have a round of applause.", he proudly stated.

Laketa and I were shocked. The pastor had arrived a few months earlier and had only attended one youth event. He stayed about fifteen minutes and stood in the corner with a stern look. He asked us if we thought the Christian rock music playing on the record player was appropriate.

He never came again and never spoke to us about stepping down. His daughter loved youth group and stopped by our house to visit now and again. Also, Jim and Julie were close friends. Why would they sneak behind our backs to take the position? Laketa was overwhelmed with sadness and had to leave the sanctuary immediately. I sat stunned for a couple more minutes before following her out. We drove home mid-service and never returned to that church.

That night we got a call from Jim and Julie saying that they thought we had resigned. They weren't remotely interested in taking the position, but the pastor talked them into it. They felt terrible that our feelings had been hurt and wanted us to take the youth group back. We declined, as this was the straw that broke the camel's back for us in this church.

The pastor never called to apologize or ask us why we left the church. There were only about fifty members, so he had to notice we were missing. He also knew that he essentially "fired" us without telling us. Some of our good friends never apologized or asked why we left either. We were stunned. We told our family members that we found a church that we didn't 100% agree doctrinally with but treated us like family. I guess we were wrong.

This was one more straw on the proverbial camel's back of our evangelical fundamentalism. Paradoxically, I had begun moving towards a more liberal view of Christianity during my Bible College years. Some of the stuff just didn't make sense. The Baptist Church in Benton City was even more conservative than what we grew up with and we were struggling with many of the teachings. This was another step on the long journey of moving away from the more fundamentalist evangelical aspects of Christianity. I felt something literally break inside me. I was tired of the fire and brimstone, tired of trying to do more and be better all the time, and tired of carrying the guilt. I'm not blaming this pastor. In fact, it helped us get started on our journey years before we might have, so it was a blessing in disguise. I do think he handled the situation quite poorly though. He should have spoken to us.

This was one of many opportunities in our spiritual journey where our childhood faith didn't seem to provide satisfactory answers. Facing cancer, losing loved ones, the inevitable breaking of relationships, all gave us the opportunity to learn and rethink our faith and how to be a follower of Jesus.

Richard Rohr says, "There must be, and if we are honest, there always will be at least one situation in our lives that we cannot fix, control, explain, change, or even understand... What I call "necessary suffering," is programmed into the journey. By denying our pain or avoiding our necessary falling, many of us have kept ourselves from our own spiritual depths"

He goes on to say, "In mythology, the would-be hero is always wounded. The word *innocent (innocens, 'not yet wounded')* is not a complimentary term in mythology. The *puer* is the young boy (*puella* for the young girl) who refuses to be wounded. More precisely, he refuses to recognize and suffer the wounds that are already there. He's just going to remain nice and normal so everybody will accept him... We must trust the pain and not get rid of it until we have learned its lessons."

Later in my life, I realized that I denied the pain and avoided falling until at least my mid-40s. We took a break from organized religion for a while and then began searching for more grace-oriented versions of Christianity.

A year later, we left Benton City with good memories of sunshine and water skiing, lots of friends, and with Lianne in tow. We were ready to begin a new phase of life with our two kids in Lynden, Washington.

Give the kid a break

There were only two weeks left in the school year and I had a splitting headache. For the love of God, could these third-grade kids ever be quiet for five seconds. I started to get angry and almost screamed at the top of my lungs at them. Then I decided, "It's ok to throw in the towel for the next hour." I told the kids to line up because we were going outside for an extra break. The kids all cheered and away we went. The fresh air helped.

This was the hardest class to manage in my eleven years of teaching. It was June and I was still reteaching the classroom routines. In previous years, my classes had the routines figured out by about the middle of September. We had seven teachers in third grade and generally each teacher took a few of the more behaviorally challenging kids. This particular year, close to a dozen moms had asked the principal if their challenging boy could have Mr. Morse for third grade. The principal asked me if I would be willing to do that, and true to form, I readily agreed. I empathized with noisy boys who couldn't hold still! I did take a lot of aspirin that year though.

I met with the mother of one of the boys the week before school started. She looked physically devastated. Her body language showed little hope for a better year. She said her son hated school and was having nightmares and regressing to a younger age. He had completely shut down in school in first grade and had refused to do any work for the last two years. Because his work was never done, he hadn't been out to recess more than a handful of times in the last couple of years. She just couldn't bear to go through another similar year. Her son, John, sat and listened while we met but didn't say anything.

At the end of the meeting, I turned to John and said, "Just come to school this year. You can have the year off from work and just be here. I want you to relax and enjoy school." I figured he hadn't done any work the last two years, what did we have to lose? I couldn't stand watching this if it were one of my kids.

Mom nervously agreed, he nodded, and away we went. I'm not sure his mom thought this was such a good idea but was likely desperate to try anything. In retrospect, I'm not certain I would give that advice to another teacher, but something in my gut told me to try it and I blurted it out before fully thinking through it. I suggested letting kids just sit for a month or two multiple times as a principal, but none of the teachers thought that was a good idea at all.

John sat at his desk quietly for a few days. He wasn't disruptive. In fact, compared to the other dozen noisy boys in that class, he was the perfect student. On about the fourth day, I was handing out a math practice sheet. I walked past John's desk without giving him a sheet like I always did.

He asked, "Can I do that worksheet?"

"Hmm… I'll have to think about that. Let me hand out the rest of these and then let's talk."

We talked and I agreed to let him try it, as long as he understood that he only had to do what he wanted and didn't have to finish the whole page. He agreed and got to work. When the recess bell rang, he only had a few problems left and asked if he could finish before he went out to recess. As I almost never let kids stay in from recess to finish work, I took what he had done and sent him outside. I missed about half my recesses in elementary school and rarely had the heart to keep a child in from recess. Also, I had to get to the staff room for my break, especially that year. I felt I was a better teacher when I took a break, as opposed to standing guard over kids who didn't finish their work, but needed a break, too.

Within a couple of weeks, John was doing all his work and fit right in. He was smiling and laughing at my corny third grade humor.

We moved from Lynden for my first principal job in Westport at the end of the school year. He called me eight years later to say, "thanks", and to tell me that he was a junior in high school, had a 3.2 GPA, was on the football team, had a part-time job, and was active in his church. That phone call remains one of my favorite five minutes to this day.

Occasionally, I gave myself permission to give up for an hour or two and chose another day and time to fight. This was especially helpful as a principal. It was the lucky kid who was the fourth kid that day to be sent to my office for the same offense. There was a good chance I would just chuckle and take a walk with the. I let kids do the same when they needed to, also. We all need a break now and again.

Fake it 'til You Make it

A week into my first principalship, I was hunkered in the office wondering what I was supposed to be doing in the weeks before school started. I had no idea. I was staring out the window at cloudy and gray Westport, Washington, a bustling metropolis of almost 2000 people in 1989. The sun came out about a dozen days a year here, and most days an umbrella was more like a kite. The nearest town is Grayland, and I thought it was named for the color of the sky and the water. I found out later that it was named after Captain Gray. It was the perfect descriptor for both towns and all of Gray's Harbor.

The phone rang on my district line. "This is Steve Morse, principal at Ocosta Elementary School.", I stated with authority and pride. This was a title I had owned for almost a week at the time. I still felt like a high school student answering the phone in the office for a credit, so I deepened my voice to not sound fourteen years old.

"This is the superintendent. Why are you telling the teachers that you're green and don't know what you're doing?"

"Well, I am completely green, and I don't know what I'm doing yet. I'm choosing to run with that mantra and build a culture of vulnerability and risk-taking."

"Don't tell teachers stuff like that yet. Fake it 'til you make it." Click. He could be quite clear and concise. This turned out to be fantastic advice that greatly influenced my career and life. In less than a minute, I learned more than at any five-day conference I've ever attended!

As I hung up the phone, a terrifying thought hit me smack in the gut. I realized I had been faking it ever since I started my classes to become a principal. In fact, I had been faking it since I was four years old. Was I ever going to make it, or will "fake it 'til you make it" be etched on my tombstone? I faked it with my parents, my church, my teachers, and my friends. Now, at 34 years old, my boss is telling me to fake it until I make it! I guess he didn't realize I was already one of the best fakers in the world. Spoiler alert … I'm 64, retired, and still feel like I'm faking it. Who in the heck would want to read a book I wrote?

I've determined that 99 percent of making it in life is putting one foot in front of the other, smiling, and thinking "Even if I'm not sure I can do this, I'm going to try." So, even if I never feel like I make it, I'll keep taking risks and moving forward one day at a time.

As Paulo Coelho stated, "You must be the person you have never had the courage to be. Gradually, you will discover that you are that person, but until you can see this clearly, you must pretend and invent."

When I retired, I got a card from our school counselor that said, "Now you don't have to fake it anymore." That was quite an insightful card and made me smile that she knew me so well. And she was right. While I still feel like a phony now and again, I have had to fake it much less often.

I think almost everyone feels like a fraud at times. Michelle Obama admitted to those feelings in her book, "Becoming". In fact, I have a hunch that no matter how successful people are or how exciting their life looks on Facebook, most people feel like they are faking it on occasion. Only the most self-unaware folks would be able to think they always had it all together.

I imagine I'll always have feelings of being a fraud. However, the more I try to live to my core values and try to stay humble and vulnerable, the less I will feel like I am faking it. Authenticity and vulnerability take care of a large percent of the faking. I hope to get better in both those areas. When necessary, I'm going to keep right on faking it though. Maybe I'll make it someday, but more likely, "He faked it well.", will be my epitaph.

Please leave a message at the beep

I was driving to my principal job in Westport later that fall and it was raining so hard that the windshield wipers couldn't completely clear the windows, even when set to top speed. I already had a headache. I suddenly began praying out loud, "Please God. Can I just have one day where the kids aren't going all crazy, fighting, spitting, yelling? Or maybe just for the morning if all day seems like too much to ask for?" I wondered what the drivers going the other way thought seeing me pleading with myself, hand motions and all.

The Ocosta principal job was by far the hardest job I had in my 39 years of public ed. It was a tough school out on the peninsula where it was every man and woman for him/herself. The kids were tough as nails. A few minutes after the words left my mouth, I realized that the prayer I offered might actually not be the right prayer. I pulled over and wondered what kind of prayer God might want a person to pray. I decided it was foolish and selfish to pray there would be no problems. It also would likely go into the mountain of unanswered prayers I had been compiling since childhood, as it didn't seem likely that all

600 kids would decide to be perfect one day. Maybe one of them would call a meeting the night before? Furthermore, most of them couldn't be good for five minutes even if you were holding a cake to give them at the end of that time. Due to all the childhood trauma and issues they were carrying, many of these kids were just surviving minute by minute.

I changed my prayer that morning to, "God, I don't know what today will bring, but whatever it brings give me patience, compassion, and wisdom to help in every situation I'm given. Help me slow down and be present." That seemed like a better prayer. I ended up being a principal for 24 years, and I don't recall even one problem free day. Nonetheless, when I was calmer, kinder, and more present, the days went much better, even when all heck was breaking loose. That was the part I could control and that was the part I felt better about asking God for help with.

Mother Teresa said, "I used to pray that God would feed the hungry, or do this or that, but now I pray that he will guide me to do whatever I'm supposed to do, what I can do. I used to pray for answers, but now I'm praying for strength. I used to believe that prayer changes things, but now I know that prayer changes us, and we change things."

I'm no theologian and certainly not a member of the clergy, but I did pay $5 for a ministerial license to perform weddings, so I should be able to reflect about prayer, right? As a kid, and on occasion as an adult, I used to see prayer as kind of like a Christmas list that I gave to Santa every year hoping to just get a few of the items I asked for. I always asked big, hoping for a compromise. I saw it as a chance to tell God everything I wanted. Maybe I wouldn't win the lottery, but could I at least get a raise or win a few bucks at the casino? Even as a kid, I recognized that my prayers weren't more important than someone who was in a war zone or starving to death, but God is infinite and personal, so she or he should be able to do both, right? Year by year and day by day, I'm thinking that maybe prayer should be mostly listening, being still and quiet. Maybe prayer is for getting in the flow with God to make the world a better place, not a lucky rabbit's foot.

Rachel Held Evans, author of *Searching for Sunday,* said she is often asked if she believes in prayer for healing. She said that she has seen so many good people not healed and seen so many frauds claiming to heal people that it is hard for her to believe in a healing prayer, but when she or a loved one is sick, she still prays and she believes anything is possible. That kind of sums it up for me.

When you look at wars, disease, and poverty; they seem to hit people who seem like reasonably good people and people who don't seem like particularly good people. The Bible says that the rain falls on the evil and the good. Like Mother Teresa and Rachel Held Evans, it doesn't appear God will always choose to intervene. It seems like God gave that job to us humans for the most part.

Nonetheless, like Rachel, when my loved ones are ill or having problems, I don't hesitate to pray. I believe in the mystery. I also recognize that it is extremely rare to see a miracle. God uses doctors and people who have studied hard and work hard to help us.

My mom had a good answer to this dilemma when I was eight. I had ordered a civil war army set from the back of a comic book and was afraid I would die, or Jesus would come before it got here. I was praying that the set would come that day, even though the ad said it would take seven to ten days. I wanted the post office to perform a miracle! After working in the post office for four summers I learned that it actually was a miracle if anything got through. Anyways, I asked mom if I could order it in heaven if I died. She must have wondered where she got such a whacko kid, but hey, she shouldn't have taken me to that church six or eight hours a week where all they talked about was the rapture and going to hell!

She contemplated for a minute and then stated, "I'm sure you could, but maybe when you get to heaven it won't seem that important." That is a doggone wise answer. That answer kind of helped and stuck with me.

Our perspective of what is important changes so much over time. What was important to me even ten years ago, is less important now. This was a great lesson for an eight-year old kid. When the Civil War set did come ten days later, it was total garbage anyways. I was so disappointed. I thought for $2.99 for 100 soldiers they would be awesome.

Like almost all of my fundamentalist childhood beliefs, my concept of prayer has changed a lot over the years, but I still pray. Like Mother Teresa said, it changes us. It makes us more thankful, helps us let go, and encourages us to alleviate suffering and help the world.

And, as my mother-in-law always says, "It can't hurt."

Racing past the harbor

The speedometer on our station wagon hit 85 mph. I was roaring down a secluded stretch of road on the way from Westport to the hospital in Aberdeen. Laketa was in the seat next to me bleeding profusely and weeping. She was pregnant and the doctor had warned her that she might lose the baby earlier that week. When we arrived, there was no heartbeat.

Laketa was heartbroken. I was also incredibly sad, but I was still at the stage of my fundamentalism where I thought denial and putting on a happy face was the right answer to every problem. After all, we had two wonderful, adopted children, many people around the world have it much worse, and we both had good jobs and caring friends. I believed my faith expected me to take it in stride and carry on happily, as an example to others. How wrong I was.

I've grown and learned a lot in the last thirty years and feel absolutely sick about how I handled this. I wounded Laketa deeply and hurt myself in the process, also. I didn't realize just how much I had hurt Laketa until she told me many years later. I thought I was being strong for her and for our kids, was living my faith, was being a "man". I wish I could have a redo and let the tears flow freely, listen quietly, and just say "I'm so sorry. I'm so sad." It is a loss I cannot regain to this day, but I'm taking the time to mourn recently, and it has been healing. We only know what we know when we know it, I guess, but this one hurt.

Tortoise and the Hare

As I got to the bottom of the stairs, I noticed my heart was pounding. I doubted this was the type of pounding that runners were seeking to improve their heart health. Seems like this type wouldn't be too healthy. I also wondered what message I was sending to parents, staff, and students to see a principal racing from place to place like there was always a fire to put out. Did that make me look like I was really a hard worker or like a fool. I hadn't yet realized that better prioritization was the way to work a 40-45-hour work week, not increased speed, and high blood pressure.

I strolled casually to the office and located a stopwatch. This was in the stone-age before everyone had an I-phone. Definite upgrade over a sundial though. I pressed start and walked as quickly as I could to the farthest classroom in the building and wrote down the time. I then pressed start and strolled leisurely back to the office. The difference was less than thirty seconds. A great example of penny wise and pound foolish. What was I giving up in terms of long-term health, the culture of our school, my success as a school administrator, my own experience as I walk through life, and modeling for students and staff to save thirty seconds a dozen times a day. It reminded me of the guy who passed me revving his engine and then sat in front of me at the next light. I made an immediate decision to slow my walk significantly. It took a little practice, but I soon mastered the skill and loved it.

Many of the teachers and parents thought something was wrong with me. "Are you okay, Steve? We're worried about you. You seem to have really slowed down recently."

I told the staff and parents what I was doing and encouraged them to try slowing their walking speed. One teacher who I saw tearing down the hall like she was in the Indy 500, slowed down every time she saw me and said, "This is difficult, but I'm trying to walk slower and it really helps the times I can remember."

I was the principal at Silver Beach Elementary in Bellingham, at this time. We had several great years in Westport and had relocated to Bellingham. The kids were growing up and life was relatively good.

This ten minute "aha moment" changed my life. Not all at once, I am still learning to slow down, get off the hamster wheel, be more mindful, but this was a strong first step in a lifetime trek.

I was also learning the hard way that when I refused to slow down voluntarily, my body would do the job for me. Almost every time I got sick, I could point to the day/s when I was especially stressed out and racing around. During an overwhelming period, I reminded myself that it wasn't worth it to rush around to get ten percent more work done if it meant I had to give up two days staying at home sick. It was the tortoise and the Hare all over again.

Surprisingly, retirement, and now the pandemic, didn't solve this issue completely for me. In some ways, I was less rushed at work once I learned to live in the moment there! I knew I was required to stay at work a certain number of hours. I never needed to hurry.

When I first retired though, I found myself rushing to finish brushing my teeth, make the coffee, work on my book for a few minutes. There was always something else I wanted to do, like… take a nap, walk the dog, play pickleball, watch tv, sit on the deck and do nothing. I was always in a hurry to get to the next event, even if the next event was doing nothing. I thought slowing down would become easier, not harder when I retired.

One time when I was ranting about how busy I was, someone said, "Steve, be a human being, not a human doing. Work more on who you are than what you accomplish." That about knocked me off my feet. I still think about that statement all the time.

When my nephew asked his dad (Clint) what advice he could give for beginning a marriage, Clint said, "Become the best person you can. It's who you are, not what you do." That seems like wise counsel for anything we do. Life's not a checklist.

I probably would have needed a different strategy in the pit at Wall Street, but this set the perfect tone for an elementary principal. I also carved out time to eat a semi-leisurely lunch with the teachers daily. I could never talk another principal into using this strategy, but I think they missed the boat. The time spent (not wasted!) eating with the teachers helped me as much as anything I did. A nice mid-day change of pace and a chance to nip concerns in the bud through conversation.

Grocery shopping with my grandson, Cruz, is one of my favorite ways to practice this skill. We walk about 1/10 of a mile an hour while he pushes his miniature cart and asks questions every five seconds like, "What's that? What's that? What's that? What's that?" He shouts with glee when he sees a balloon or a snack box with a cartoon character he recognizes. What used to be a 20-minute heart pounding race around the store becomes a 50-minute recreational activity. It's as fun as going to the zoo. Now that I'm retired, I've got nowhere to go and all day to get there, so it's perfect! I also tend to drive slower and just enjoy the trip.

Author's warning: Purposely going slower can be dangerous if practiced in the presence of friends and family members, especially when they are in a hurry. I advise that you use these techniques when alone at first. Moving slowly when accompanied by others, especially spouses and adult children, can lead to higher blood pressure and increased tension in those accompanying you. This may also be transmitted back to you through verbal interactions or body language.

For the record, I am immensely thankful there are people willing to work 18-hour days seven days a week to find the cure for cancer, a vaccine for Covid-19, etc. Most of our great advancements would never have happened without the super achievers who rarely sleep. For most of us though, the world probably won't implode if we slow down a little and work on being human beings, rather than compiling a list of achievements.

Thich Nhat Hahn writes, "When we walk like we are rushing, we print anxiety and sorrow on the earth. We have to walk in a way that we print only peace and serenity on the earth. Be aware of the contact between your feet and the earth. Walk as if you are kissing the earth with your feet."

L word issues

"I don't know who you people are, but I sure love you.", said Mom with a huge smile. She had been living in a home for Alzheimer's patients for several months at the time. Dad visited her every day after she moved there for a couple of years. This was the first time Mom had ever told us she loved us. Even though she didn't recognize us, it still moved us to hear the L word from mom. I saw an article that claimed the things you always wanted to say pop up when you get Alzheimer's, some good and some not so good. I'm not sure if that's true, but I want to believe that she always wanted to verbalize her love and the Alzheimer's finally released her to say the words.

I had a hard time ever saying the L word, also. I think I was a good dad, but Laketa had to teach me to be more expressive to our own kids. I wasn't cold. I spent a lot of time on the floor playing with the kids, carried them around, and made them laugh constantly. However, she noticed that I seldom told them I loved them or physically hugged them. After some feedback and coaching, she put me on the right track with my own kids. This was one piece of advice I never bristled at, which is rare for me. I knew my own experiences of never hearing I was loved or being physically hugged might sidetrack me as a Dad, so I was always thankful for the reminders. I followed her lead and was soon hugging my kids and verbally expressing love.

I don't remember hearing the word "love" much before I was about 23 years old. Mom and Dad were uncomfortable verbalizing love, even though I am certain now that they loved us. It was a different era. Our family didn't hug much either. When a friend in elementary school said his mom kissed him on the cheek when she tucked him in at night, I thought that was the grossest thing I had ever heard. Yuck. I stood still like a wooden block when people hugged me until I was about twenty years old. Finally, a friend told me that it's ok to hug back. She practiced with me and showed me how to hug like a normal human being. I was a little better at reciprocating a hug after that but didn't ever initiate much.

Dad let the L word slip once on the phone in his 90's, about a year before he passed. I don't think he realized he said it.

I started tearing up and couldn't speak for a while. I finally squeaked out, "I love you, too." He acted like he didn't hear me and never said it again, even though we all said it to him every time we saw him.

Kids today seem more open to verbalizing love, as are the parents raising them. I frequently heard kids at school telling each other, "I love you". The kids even said "I love you" to their teachers and me. I kind of mumbled incoherently in return the first few years, but finally got over my fears and just said, "I love you, too, friend." This made the kids beam and no one accused me of being inappropriate, as I never initiated the greeting.

Cruz hears "I love you." about five times an hour. When we were leaving the library one morning, Cruz turned to a group of kids and parents he had been playing with and yelled, "Bye, I love you." The parents all laughed heartily and yelled back, "We love you, too."

I didn't fully realize until about ten years ago that the lack of intimacy from my parents is likely what made intimacy so problematic for me. I would have been a better spouse and father with more intimacy. I invariably keep a wall around me to some degree. I have a lot of friends, even close friends, but generally seem to hold something back. I suppose that is not unique among males from my generation, but I'm trying to get better.

When Dad was in his 70's one of my sibs asked him why he never told us or mom that he loved us. He replied, "I don't need to say it. I showed you every day by going to work and being here."

I'm improving and getting lots of practice with Cruz. My siblings and I recently spent a weekend together, just the four of us, for the first time in our lives, and I even used the L word with my sibs. Tremendous progress for a crusty old guy like me. I'll likely end up one of those sappy, old grandpas. Oh well, that's fine with me.

Marital Advice 101

About six or seven years into our marriage, I asked a friend what the key was to his seemingly strong marital relationship. These two seemed to support and care about each other. They listened respectfully when the other was speaking and were on the same page with priorities. I never once sensed irritation or tension between them. I assumed they must be really working hard behind the scenes to make things work so smoothly. Maybe they had checklists for their relationships and a daily meeting. I wanted to incorporate a few of the key strategies they were using.

He replied, "You need to lower your expectations." I almost fell to the floor laughing, as this was the opposite of what I expected him to say. Where was his reading list? Did they have goals with weekly check-ins? And what do you mean by lower my expectations? Can't I be the best at work, exercise daily, go back in the evenings to get my master's degree, volunteer, attend church, be a good friend, be an exceptional parent and still have an exceptional marital relationship? That seemed to be the message I was getting from everyone else. Are you on to something here?

Also, even if I did decide to hold ridiculously high expectations of myself, is it fair to expect that of my spouse? Even if/when I eventually crash at some point, it was my own choice. However, when I have unreasonable expectations of my spouse, friends, and co-workers, it wasn't their choice. If I have unrealistic expectations of my spouse and those closest to me, they will only be willing to feel like a disappointment for so long before they walk away from our relationship.

Giving people the grace to grow and the acceptance of where they are at any given time is the best thing I learned as an adult. It saved my marriage, made me a better parent, principal, and human being. As a kid who grew up feeling like my mom was disappointed in me every day of my life, I should have known better than to pass that on. It's interesting how human beings tend to pass on our childhood experiences, good and bad. No matter how determined we are to be different, breaking the cycle is difficult. I'm beyond thankful that, for the most part, I reversed course in this area. People generally consider me a non-judgmental person.

Over thirty years later, this is still the best marital relationship advice I received. Laketa and I read about seven or eight books before and following our wedding. We attended premarital counseling and short periods of therapy a few times during our marriage, but I learned more from Terry in a few seconds. We both lowered our expectations of each other and attempted to love each other unconditionally at whatever stage we were at. After four decades, we're still hanging in there and giving each other grace. Our marriage is far from perfect, but we both have someone who knows us intimately and still loves unconditionally.

Principals and supervisors who work seventy hours a week and disdain employees who don't follow their lead are rarely successful leaders. I have nothing against being the best and my work and personal life have been oriented to continuous improvement. However, I believe we must prioritize and can't be the best at everything. Personal and institutional change are incremental. An accepting day to day journey of continual improvement is the best path forward.

Dad was a great example of acceptance. He didn't show much

emotion and was kind of absent at times, but I always felt like he knew I'd turn out okay. I think my sibs would agree. There was an attitude of, "You're all going to turn out just fine.", behind the silence. This stood in stark juxtaposition to some of my friends who had dads' who verbally ripped them to shreds.

When the school called to tell dad what a pain I was, he didn't express disappointment or shame me. He took the opposite approach. He would pull me aside to let me know that he was confident I could solve this problem myself. That was the end of the conversation, and he never checked back in. He hated conflict, so part of that strategy may have been his aversion to conflict, but it made me believe I could handle it myself. He gave me a quiet confidence that helped to overcome my negative self-talk. I felt better after these conversations and I knew I would turn out fine, too. Unfortunately for my teachers though, his strategy wasn't effective in getting me to behave, because even though I *knew* that I "could" handle it, I didn't have any interest in handling it at that time. My long-range plan was to savor the laughs and turn it around the last month or two of my senior year. Seemed like the perfect strategy. What could possibly go wrong?

Dad never pressured us to become doctors or lawyers and he tried to talk me out of going to college. He never told us a B wasn't good enough. I appreciated that about him. Reaching our potential never came up in conversation. If we stayed out of jail and had a job, he was happy as a clam! While I don't agree with that parenting philosophy completely, it's probably better than some of the helicopter parents who stress their kids out by expecting nothing but the absolute best in karate, piano, violin, ballet, math, science, ASB president, ... you get the point. Balance seems to be a key in almost every facet of life. Nonetheless, we all seemed to turn out "ok, kind of".

After Dad turned about 75, he used to get teary eyed when we all gathered as a family. Even though he still couldn't quite choke out the "L word", he was becoming much more emotionally aware. He would bang his glass for quiet and announce in a shaky voice, "I'm so proud of each and every one of you. "You all have jobs and none of you are in jail." We used to respond with a combination of tears in our eyes at his pride and laughing uproariously about the low expectations. Although, the jury has been out for each of us at different junctures of our lives and the wolf is always at the door, he's been right so far.

In the words of Rachel Marie Martin, "Sometimes you have to let go of the picture of what you thought life would be like and learn to find joy in the story you are actually living."

I had to decide what was the most important to me and prioritize those values. That gave me the freedom to lower my expectations in some areas. I also had to give other people the time and grace to grow at their own speed. I couldn't expect any relationship or career choice to be perfect. Once I learned to bring those expectations down a notch or two, life was better.

D'oh

I was relaxing around the campfire one night in the early 90's with Dana when he told a story about a Simpsons episode he had recently seen. When I replied that I never seen an episode, he was appalled.

"You're kidding! What is wrong with you. It's the best show on tv." I was still in a fundamentalist mindset at the time and I told him it just didn't seem like a good way to spend my time. Oh, brother. A little self-righteous, maybe? He convinced me to give it a shot. I was never a master at resisting peer pressure, so I agreed to try it.

The first episode I almost fell off the couch laughing. It matched my own sense of humor closely. I have always believed that you can't take life too seriously, and I loved the way the show made fun of every institution equally. When I look closely at the schools, the church, the government, the family, the neighborhood, or myself ... situations make me chuckle out loud multiple times an hour all day long. I laugh at stuff in my head without anyone speaking. D'oh became my well-known catchphrase at work and with friends from that point on. Whenever I say, "D'oh.", around Cruz he asks me, "What's D'oh, Papa?", so I'm getting lots of chances to teach him subtle humor at a young age. He'll know just the right time to use that phrase.

Laketa worked as a church secretary at the same church we attended for a few years in Bellingham. She enjoyed the job and the pastor was a nice guy. The first day Joel attended youth group in middle school, the youth group leader had the kids sit in a circle for an icebreaker. The first question was, "What is your favorite tv show."

The kids all laughed, thinking Joel was joking around when he answered, "The Simpsons." Either they weren't watching the Simpsons by sixth grade or they were all little suck-ups.

The leader asked Joel, "What would your parents say if I called and told them this was your favorite show?" He must have thought we were more religious than we were, due to Laketa working at the church.

Joel could be a bit of a smart aleck. I don't know where he picked that up. Probably the public schools. Joel replied, "Sure. Give Dad a call. I'm not sure what he will say, but I can tell you this. At about seven o'clock every night, he yells at me to hurry up and get downstairs because the Simpsons is starting.".

I laughed so hard when Joel told the story, but Laketa wasn't nearly as amused. Watching the Simpsons regularly with Joel is an area that we didn't have complete agreement on, but she responded with a "we'll see how that works out" attitude. Lianne wasn't quite interested enough to join us very often but did occasionally. In retrospect, she probably made the wiser choice of how to spend her time.

While I was extremely passionate and serious about my principal role, I also laughed my head off most days. The kids pulled some hilarious stuff. One time, one of our toughest six-year-old boys was sitting in the hall in an "off-limits area" about half an hour before school started. I could tell by the look on his face that this wasn't the day to make removing him from quietly sitting in the hall my top priority. A teacher and I walked by and sincerely said, "Good morning, Don, we are glad that you came today." He looked up and flipped us the bird with both hands and then put his head back down. We walked around the corner and almost fell over trying not to snort loudly enough for him to hear. It wasn't really that humorous, but just one of those moments. He ended up having a fantastic day at school, and I might have ended up in a six-hour war had I chose to try to move him out of the hall at that moment

Another time, a third-grade girl went into the coat closet in her classroom and announced to her 22-year old second week on the job male teacher that she had taken all her clothes off. He came racing down to the office in a panic. Jolynda, the secretary, just chuckled and calmly told him to take the rest of his class for a walk while she coaxed the young lady out of the closet and got her dressed. I overheard the conversation and was cracking up at my desk. I didn't let on that I had overheard. Better for JoLynda to handle that one. We all had a good belly laugh that day about the poor teacher. Welcome to Roosevelt! Did they teach you this one in college?

We usually had several amusing kid stories every day. While situations similar to these aren't "funny" in a typical way, as it is also sad to see students with trauma, it seemed better to chuckle and carry on than spend every day running around under a giant storm cloud with furrowed brows. Parents, kids, and teachers noticed a huge change in positive climate after I arrived. I've worked with principals and teachers who act like they are on the front lines in Syria every day. I think that's unhealthy for kid, teachers, and parents. When the boss can lighten up, laugh a little, and not make every situation into an emergency it's more pleasant for everyone. I see no advantage to treating every situation like the end of the world.

Irony abounded in education. One of the most ironic experiences was repeated on a regular basis when parents threatened to sue us because their child wasn't getting extra help. Ironically, this was usually after refusing any extra help for several years because they didn't want their child to be singled out. It was tough to get too upset about that one. All I could do was chuckle in my head and carry on. If you can't smile at least a little bit at some of these of situations, you'll either have a short or miserable career as a school administrator. And, if you expect situations like that to never happen, you'll be in for a big surprise over time.

Some of the managerial type decisions made by our administrative team were also laugh out loud hilarious. I often pointed these out at our monthly meetings, but my first boss seldom appreciated it as much as I expected. Unfortunately for my career aspirations, a few people usually snickered, and that was enough to keep me going. My last boss greatly appreciated it though. He encouraged me to keep it coming numerous times, as he felt it helped break the tension of a serious job.

Most importantly of all, I laugh at myself about 50 times a day. If I couldn't laugh at myself, my profession, my church, or my community, I'd be in for a long haul. Life's too short and there is too much pain in this world to not have a good belly laugh now and again. I probably laugh too much, but that's the side I prefer to err on.

As Anne Lamott says, "Laughter is carbonated holiness. Find people who laugh gently at themselves, who remind you gently to lighten up."

That's all the time I have for this chapter. The Simpsons is starting in two minutes and I have to keep developing my sense of satire and irony. I wish Joel still lived at home.

You're welcome

"This is the third musical I've seen, and it was the best yet. Thank you so much, Mr. Morse."

"I didn't really do anything. The teachers and students did all the work. I just tried to stay out of the way.", I replied to the tenth person in a row as parents filed out of the auditorium.

My response left the parents uncomfortable and unsure what to say next. It also usually removed the smile from their face. I needed to learn a new response.

My parents taught me to say "thank you" as a young pup. They required me to handwrite thank you letters as a kid, with no computer or email. I was proficient at thanking people. I wasn't as competent at accepting compliments or saying, "you're welcome."

It seems many people struggle verbalizing these two words. It was particularly difficult after I became a principal, as usually the less involved I was in major events the better the events turned out. I could often honestly say, "I didn't do much.", for most of our open houses, etc. Once I learned to simply say only two words though, "You're welcome.", and nothing else, it became a more satisfying experience for both of us.

I know I appreciated it when I gave a kid or teacher a compliment and they looked me in the eyes and said, "Thank you, Mr. Morse." Short and sweet. It gave me joy. It was easier said than done, but life-changing to learn to accept a compliment graciously and with few words.

SECOND WIND
... 1993-2013

A new beginning

I was at a point where I was ready for a change when the district asked me to transfer to Roosevelt Elementary. It was hard to leave Silver Beach, as I had grown close to the community. However, I was excited about the challenges at Roosevelt. My supervisor informed me that the climate had recently become negative, the teachers were discouraged, and the kids were out of control. Parents were upset and had been pressing the superintendent and the board to pour extra money and support to the school. This was exactly the type of job I had been looking for. My skill set of making school fun, staying calm, connecting with kids, and encouraging teachers seemed like the right combination to at least give it a shot. This next section will be about my time at Roosevelt and what I was learning. I also included a few family/personal lessons that came about during this time.

Before beginning my time at Roosevelt, I had been reading a lot about the many educational inequities our country was facing. Poor and minority students were not faring well. Roosevelt had a relatively high poverty, high minority, and high English as a Second Language student population, and I was eager to get in there and see if I could help make a difference. This transfer and my desire to make a difference with historically vulnerable populations kept me passionate about my career right to the end. I enjoyed every year and was proud to end my career as the Civil Rights Director for the district.

Often principals accept a job at a high poverty school under the premise that they are going to come in with guns blazing to fix these kids. They choose a standardized "back to the basics" no frills/boring curriculum, cancel field trips, and cut recess time. They bring a stern demeanor and no-tolerance for any nonsense, like the guy with the baseball bat in the movie. Really? You gonna hit a kid with that?

Personally, I believed that was 180 degrees the wrong approach. These were the kids who most needed fun, hope, love, and joy. Public schools often submit the kids with the least exposure to the arts and travel to more sitting, less recess, art, field trips and music. They also often have sterner "no tolerance" discipline policies. How is this going to reach the hardest to reach students?

I decided to take the opposite approach. For the assembly the first morning, rather than coming out in a suit and tie to give a stern message about how things were going to be different around here, I swung out on a rope in a Tarzan outfit to blasting music. I ran behind a partition and changed costumes several times pretending to be the new principal with a different goofy costume each time. When I ran out, the PE teacher interrupted me after a few minutes addressing the student body to say, "Wait a minute. You're not the new principal. Go back there and get the real one!" I finally came out as the "real principal" in my shorts and flip flops. I told the kids how much fun we were going to have this year and that I couldn't wait to meet them all. I still smile every time I remember some of the teacher's faces at the assembly. To their credit though, they jumped right onboard and were willing to give a new approach a try!

I excused the younger kids and then sat on the gym floor with the fourth and fifth grade kids and told them how much I needed their help as leaders and role models. We were in this together to make Roosevelt the best school in town. I continued meeting with them for a few months to elicit their help and support. Most were happy to help, even the tough guys and gals. And guess what, our kids and families thought we were the best school in town. We started getting student and teacher transfer requests to come to our school from other areas.

Roosevelt was by far my favorite principal gig. I was experienced enough to give myself full permission to be more myself. Teachers, staff, parents, and kids all loved the school. We had weekly assemblies where the teachers and I would dress up and do funny skits. I jumped off a ladder into a kiddy pool, rode a motorcycle through the gym, swung in on a rope dressed as different characters, fell off a skateboard and did all kinds of crazy stunts. Of course, I told the kids not to try any of these idiotic things at home. As if any kid listens to that kind of advice though.

I interrupted class regularly with dumb announcements, usually in an Irish accent. I also had a closet full of outfits including bath robes, slippers, wigs, old man, and old lady clothes that I used at assemblies, or just put on and wandered around the halls pretending to be lost

I felt fully accepted and loved/appreciated here. I learned a great deal every day. This changed the arc of my career.

Support the troops

I was listening to the radio when I heard an advertisement for a company where the owner said something to the effect of, "We are a great place to work. We have the best and happiest employees. If you shop here, you will be treated like a king by our employees. I believe that treating my employees well is even more important than treating the customers well, as the employees will carry being treated well over to the customers."

This really resonated with me. I believed treating the teachers well, encouraging, and empowering them, was the most important thing I could do, also. That seemed like the optimal way to improve any school.

Hearing that people were discouraged when I came to Roosevelt, I made it my goal to immediately triple down to support and encourage them. It was easy to do because they were great human beings who cared about kids and worked hard. Interestingly, Clint felt the same way in a business setting. I'll let him describe it.

Clint
<u>Are employees more important than our customers?</u>
My answer is yes, for one reason: without great employees, Mosaic cannot serve their customers well. Without satisfied customers, we'd soon be out of business altogether.

At the outset, I had a few great people around me who helped start Mosaic. Since then, our staff has mushroomed to over 250 people. In as much as they are employees, they are also my valued peers, and I respect them deeply. In many ways I consider them the authentic stakeholders (owners if you will) of Mosaic. We've been through hard-fought battles and red-eye plane flights together; marooned by bad weather and frustrated by difficult situations. We've bonded during family crises and business downturns, during ecstatic successes and mind-numbing fatigue. We have each other's back and hold true to each other.

Through it all, I have made a conscious decision to treat our employees the way I'd like to be treated - with respect and dignity in how we manage, grace in difficult times, good pay, solid benefits, generous vacation and sick days, – and fun; picnics, parties and even pet insurance[RC1]. We help, support, and respect each other every bit as much as we do our clients. Once you experience working in harmony and synchronicity, it's highly addictive. We don't worry about employee turnover because people tend to stick around. And we're genuinely happy they're here.

Steve again
Like Clint, I felt that if leadership supports the employees completely and fully, they will support the customer exceptionally well. Obviously, we were all in it for the kids and the kids' success is the most important *outcome*. However, the best way by far for the principal to help achieve that outcome is to prioritize the teachers. In my day to day work, my work with the teachers was exponentially more critical than my work with any individual student.

A new parent told me she could tell we had a great school. I found this interesting, because she had asked to meet with me over her concerns when she transferred from a high socio-economic school with higher test scores. I chuckled and asked her how she could tell, as her kids had only been at Roosevelt a couple of days. She claimed that she felt positive about the school the day she registered her kids, and after walking them to class the first two days she was convinced of it. The way adults and kids interacted with each other, the smiles, kids opening doors and welcoming her family. She added that her kids came home from school thrilled the first two days and already had new friends. They couldn't wait to go back. Most of our parents felt the same way.

Substitute teachers regularly stopped by to meet with me at the end of the day. We had so many students with problematic behaviors that I expected a complaint about a kid. More often than not though, the subs wanted to tell me what a nice place Roosevelt was. They told me that almost every kid and staff member said hello and smiled at them in the halls. Kids opened doors for them and offered to help carry things. Teachers asked if they needed anything and gave specific helpful offers such as, "If Johnny is refusing to work, send him next door to my room and I'll let him work there for a while, talk to him, and send him back. If he continues to struggle, he can just spend the rest of the day with me. He has a hard time with a change in routine." Many of these subs had been warned previously that this was a problematic neighborhood and to expect a long day. This made me swell with pride every single time it happened.

By valuing employees, even more than the customers, I was able to help create a climate that worked for everyone. Customers come and go, students and families come and go, but the employees are the heart that makes the school or company what it is.

"I've learned that people will forget what you said, people will forget what you did, but people will never forget how you made them feel. "– Maya Angelou

"A sign you have a positive workplace culture is laughter... You can work hard and still laugh." - Sam Glenn

To thine own self be true
A kid came running into my office. "Mr. Morse. Hurry, we need you in the choir room." A fifth-grade girl had punched another girl in the face during the final choir practice and was sitting on the floor refusing to report to the office.

There was a choir performance that night and fifth grade graduation was only three days away. We had a no-tolerance policy for that degree of physical aggression, and the choir director correctly informed Katie that she wouldn't be able to attend the concert that night and would probably be suspended the final three days of school. I called her parents, but I had to leave a message.

About ten minutes after school let out, I got a call from her dad asking if she could sing in the concert and finish the final three days of her elementary school career. Her grandparents had driven hundreds of miles to see the concert and attend the fifth-grade graduation. Katie had been looking forward to the concert and graduation for weeks. She had struggled through a difficult elementary school experience and he wanted her to finish strong. Her dad didn't complain that it was unfair or assert that she hadn't punched the girl, he just pleaded for mercy. I told him I needed some time to think and would call him back, as I knew the teacher generally needed to hold the line with 120 kids in the choir. I also knew that she would back any decision I made and had the same values I had around looking out for the under-dog. I definitely wanted to talk to her first though.

My stomach physically hurt thinking about this family and her grandparents sitting around unhappy for the next five days. It went against my intuition to not show mercy, even though I had held the line plenty of times by this point of my principal career. Holding the line goes with the territory. However, this situation felt different to me. What did we have to lose with three days left? This appeared to be an opportunity to model extreme grace to Katie's family, and the Roosevelt community of teachers, families, and kids. I could meet with the kids and the teachers to explain my thinking. I think they would under-stand. I was also more than willing to take the blame with any upset kids or parents who wouldn't be expecting to see her that evening. I could take the heat off the choir teacher.

I called Katie's parents back to inform them her suspension was rescinded, and she could sing that night, if they drove her to the concert instead of riding the bus. Furthermore, I told them she could return to school the last three days as my assistant principal, but that she couldn't return to class. That compromise protected the other kids and showed mercy to her.

The concert was a huge success, as always, and Katie sang her heart out. I teared up a bit watching her sing and watching her proud family and grandma in the audience. The last three days turned out kind of fun, too. Peer issues had made school problematic for Katie most of the time she was at Roosevelt. She was finally able to relax, smile, and enjoy the days. She almost looked like a different kid. We had a blast roving around the school, and she was helpful many times with younger kids who just needed someone to talk to or play with when they had hurt feelings.

I fondly remember the hug from Katie and the tears in all our eyes after fifth grade graduation. And guess what, the choir director didn't lose control of her 100+ student choir in future years just because we didn't hold the line that one time! Sometimes I think schools worry too much about what the other kids will think when we make exceptions, rather than what is the best for that particular kid. When I met with the choir kids on Monday, they all seemed fine with the decision and it gave them a new way to think about situations when someone makes that type of mistake. Also, they didn't have to worry about her bothering anyone, as she was with me until graduation. I couldn't have held my ground in this case just to prove a point and still felt like I was Steve Morse.

I'm not Spike Lee, but I always tried to do the right thing, regardless of the politics or district leadership at the time. There were many times when I wasn't 100 percent sure what the right thing actually was, especially in my principal and parental roles. In those situations, I attempted to stay true to myself and lean on the values of compassion, looking out for the underdog, etc. I'm confident I wasn't always right, but I held my core values.

I wish I had known myself better at a younger age. You can't be true to yourself unless you know yourself. And to know yourself, you need to slow down and self-reflect. I was always too busy, and my mind was on the hamster wheel. I would have been a better parent, principal, and person had I known myself earlier. If I'm ever a dictator in a small country, I am going to require everyone to go to counseling and yoga. I'll also give everyone a free hot tub!

I never really understood the phrase, "To thine own self be true", growing up, but I sure see the value now. A couple guys I met in college often proclaimed, "Know thyself. To thine own self be true.", anytime they thought the situation warranted it. They attempted a British accent and they were sort of pompous asses, but now at least I know why this quote was so famous.

I'm no Shakespeare expert, but I often find myself thinking that William was right. The more I know myself and stay true to myself, regardless of what is going on around me, I will be on the right path. "To thine own self be true" is a great motto. I just hope I don't start saying it all the time with a faux British accent. If I do, please walk up behind me, and hit me in the back of the head with a 2x4 when I'm not looking. Thanks!

- "The intelligent come to know the world. The wise come to know themselves." – James Pierce/Philosopher's Bar

You're a good man, Charlie Brown

"You're a good egg, Steve Morse."

The principal intern told me that one day as she was heading out the door to talk to a kid at recess. It gave me pause. That compliment made me happy. People seldom give those type of compliments. Educational experts are always telling us that we should praise kids only for effort or an action, not for who they are. Principals were told the same for teachers. We weren't supposed to say, "You're a good man, Charlie Brown.", in a 21st century school.

I agree with the experts that saying something like, "I really like the way you don't give up.", is much better than saying, "You are so smart! I attempted to be as specific as possible with praise to both kids and adults. Generic praise like "good job" is much less helpful than specific praise. It's the same with criticism. Telling an athlete to bend her knees before shooting a free throw is much better than just saying "bad shot". When you aren't specific and don't let kids know that they can improve with effort, kids start to see themselves in the binary of good/bad, smart/dumb. Kids need to understand that their work ethic and willingness to keep trying are important traits and something they can control.

Telling kids how smart and special they are doesn't work all that well either and may lead to an attitude of entitlement. It also causes kids to give up quickly if they don't understand something. They are either smart or not. We need to teach a growth mindset where everyone can improve and emphasize the correlation between work and outcomes.

So, now that the "experts" know that I understand the basic concept, can I just say … I believe that we took this way too far my last several years in education. It was like the word police were watching in case we used non-specific praise. I hated that.

Sometimes I just kneeled down, looked a kid right in the eyes and said, "I like you just the way you are. You're a good kid." They beamed and walked away proudly. It feels validating to be told you're a good guy now and again. Everything doesn't have to be a specific compliment for something you did well. The "good egg" comment felt good, even though it didn't specifically tell me exactly what I was doing to be an effective principal or how I could improve.

As evaluators, we were instructed to never tell a teacher they are doing something well or poorly. We were supposed to describe in detail the competency that they were demonstrating so that they can either improve or know they have met that competency. A robot could have done the evaluations.

I could never do the observations that way. My supervisor was probably thrilled the day I retired. We only do one or two formal observations and evaluations a year, so I typically used that time to tell teachers what they were doing well. I broke the most important rule of non-specific feedback the minute our post-evaluation conversation began by saying, "You're a good teacher and a good human being. I'm proud to work with you and glad you are at this school."

When I had concerns about a teacher's performance, I broached these concerns outside of the formal evaluation process, at least until it became an "official" problem. I had those conversations the same day I noticed an issue and then used the more formal process for more general feedback.

Lord knows I would have loved to hear that I was a "good kid" once or twice in elementary school. A couple of my teachers even went so far as to tell me the first time I entered the room in September that they had heard what a bad kid I was from last year's teacher. They made sure I knew I wasn't going to get away with anything in their room.

Talk about throwing down the gauntlet. I seem to remember thinking, "Game on. Let's see how you do, old man (or old woman)." This is another one of those moments that feels like it happened this morning. I think I proved them wrong every year and left elementary school undefeated! My fourth-grade teacher even had to leave mid-year after suffering a nervous breakdown. That one wasn't all my fault though. There were about six other knuckleheads like me in the room. I'm not sure how her class got so loaded. Maybe the principal was hoping she would quit that year.

When a sparkling enthusiastic brand-new teacher was hired to replace her midyear, the principal took us seven idiots outside the classroom and had the new teacher perform a preemptive strike. She was required to give each of us a swat before starting her tenure. We lined up and worked our way through an assembly line process. Her heart wasn't in it though, and the principal made her perform do-overs when she didn't whack us hard enough.

This didn't turn out to be an award-winning strategy. We continued to be about equally naughty immediately upon returning to class. We laughed and bragged at recess that the swats didn't hurt a bit. However, she finished the year, so maybe it was just the ticket. Maybe the principal received national recognition for a speech entitled, "The value of preemptive strikes in handling juvenile delinquency. Strike first, before they have a chance to act out!"

For those of you thinking, "As a lifelong educator, doesn't that make you feel bad that the teacher had a nervous breakdown?"

As a kid my attitude was, ... "You're getting paid for this, you're a grown ass adult, I'm getting tons of positive peer reinforcement, and you're mean as a snake. Plus, you were the one throwing down the gauntlet on day one." Tormenting teachers rarely bothered me much at all.

Nonetheless, in this case, I felt and still feel terrible. I almost couldn't include this anecdote in the book because I don't want to look like such a horrible human being. She was one of the kindest teachers I had in elementary school and we ran over the top of her like a steamroller. She cried most days before she left, and I felt lousy every single time she wept.

Nonetheless, that didn't seem to change my behavior. I'm not sure I had the skills I needed to make a change, and I'd place a bet in Vegas that I had undiagnosed ADHD. I always felt as if I wanted to leap right out of my skin and couldn't be quiet or hold still for ten seconds, even if you held a gun to my head. I hope this kind teacher landed on her feet at another school.

If you are out there and remember your first teaching assignment and a little guy named Steve, please forgive me. I wasn't trying to ruin anyone's life. I was just trying to make the school experience more enjoyable for the 25 kids fortunate enough to be in the same class as I every year! Please e-mail me, so I can apologize personally.

Anyways, how did I get so far off topic? I'm trying to remember what this section is about. Oh yeah, I was wishing I had heard, "You're a good kid.", more growing up and not always been told how bad I was. Specifically, this chapter is about the importance of telling yourself and others that you/they are a good person, for no specific reason at all! Not for something you or they did.

As a child, I was taught the first step to becoming a Christian was to admit I was a horrible sinner with a black heart. I bought fully into the concept, even though at age five, I hadn't murdered anyone yet, and wasn't too sure what I had done that was so terrible. (For the record, I still haven't murdered anyone yet, that was just an example. Please don't notify the authorities.) I stayed stuck on that first step of Christianity for a long time and didn't move on to the, "God loves you just the way you are.", part of the deal until adulthood. I would have loved it if someone at home or school had just looked me in the eyes as a kid and said, "Steve Morse. You are a good boy. I really like you." I personally witnessed how powerful that statement was hundreds and hundreds of times over forty years as an educator.

It was much easier telling others they were "good people" than telling myself I was a good guy. I talk to myself on the radio show in my head about sixteen hours a day. Doesn't everyone? A good percent of my self-talk is straight from my childhood. "You are the dumbest principal/tennis player/handyman/parent/person I've ever met or even heard of." I'm attempting to rewire my brain to change my self-talk. And it's slowly working! I'm doing better.

PS: This works well with dogs, too. I get a kick out of watching Tyson's tail wag when I tell him what a good boy he is. Researchers claim that dogs love hearing those two words. Allegedly, the authors of the books written to read to your dog include this phrase many times.

PSPS: If you ever hear I am reading Tyson a bedtime story every night, please sneak up behind me and smack me in the back of the head with that same 2x4 one more time. Tyson has no trouble falling asleep without a bedtime story. In fact, he sleeps about 22 hours a day.

"You're a good guy, Steve Morse. Don't be so doggone hard on yourself." – Steve Morse, speaking to self in a speech recorded on his couch in Birch Bay. - June 2020.

Do What you Can

When I was working at Roosevelt I felt as if I could never even get close to solving all the problems that students, families, and a few teachers brought to school with them. That made me wonder how we would ever get even close to solving the problems in our city, county, and world. It could be discouraging. Learning to live one day/moment at a time and do what I could in that moment was the only solution I could come up with.

Dorothy Day (1897-1980), the founder of the Catholic Worker, wrote, "Young people say, what good can one person do? What is the sense of our small effort? They cannot see that we must lay one brick at a time, take one step at a time; we can be responsible only for the one action of the present moment."

I learned to move forward incrementally with the knowledge that we had an imperfect system, while picking off an initiative or two at a time and planting a few seeds for future initiatives.

As Michelle Obama wrote, "Change is equal parts patience and rigor and sometimes we have to learn to live with reality while in the midst of making progress."

I gave Michelle's advice to teachers and parents numerous times. The balance of patience and rigor, while living in reality, is a tough target to hit. Looking back, I wonder if I was too slow about some issues. It was certainly easier to solve individual issues than school-wide issues, and I did that often. For instance, completely changing school culture to be antiracist takes longer than helping one kid/family at a time. I could help the one kid immediately, while working towards a more equitable culture takes longer.

I usually felt like the kid on the beach with thousands of starfish, throwing them back one at a time. When the man says, "You'll never save them all.", the kid replies, "I saved that one." I learned to be able to sleep at night by doing what I could in the moment.

Find a sheep
One day a teacher ran down to the office to report that Michael, the new kid in second grade, had plugged the sinks in the restroom and a river was running down the hallway.

I hurried to the scene and in my firmest principal voice said something like, "We don't do that here, Michael. Let's talk. I'll help you with whatever is bothering you."

His response was something along the lines of, "F*** you and this school. No one tells me what to do."

Well, there you go. I guess that set me in my place. That wasn't the response I was expecting, but I'd heard similar responses many times before and I wasn't too shocked. I had successfully managed these conversations in the past. However, after about ten more minutes of trying to solve this one, the water had spread all the way down the hall, so there was a greater sense of urgency than usual for a plan B.

I decided to try my best principal voice and body language again. "All right, Michael. That is enough. If you don't turn off the water before I count to three, I'm coming in and turning it off."

"Come on in. I'll tell my momma you molested me in the bathroom."

Hmmm... this kid was pretty good. At this point in my principal career, I rarely met my match. I had convinced kids to come out from under at least a hundred tables and even a bus one time!

Plan C was for the custodian and I each to grab a mop and bucket while the secretary called his mom to come get him. He became my sheep for the next couple of years. We spent a lot of time together and became quite close. Let me explain.

Stephen Covey uses the Biblical parable of the 99 sheep and the one as the basis for one of his "7 Habits of Highly Effective People." His book and this parable heavily influenced my life and work. I prioritized finding the one kid who had gone astray to bring back to the flock. It usually ended up being at least a dozen kids, but the concept is finding the lost "one".

I believed this was the right thing to do in my life work and lived by the Paul Shane Spear quote, "As one person I cannot change the world, but I can change the world of one person."

Henri Nouwen was a great example of this. After nearly two decades of being an author and teaching at academic institutions including Notre Dame, Yale, and Harvard, he decided to work with individuals with extreme intellectual and developmental disabilities one on one. To him, his life work was about more than reaching a wide audience.

George Boyle, the Jesuit priest who founded Homeboy Industries says, "It would seem that, quite possibly, the ultimate measure of health in any community might reside in our ability to stand in awe at what folks have to carry rather than in judgment at how they carry it."

I wanted Roosevelt to be the same way. I didn't want our families, kids, and teachers harshly judging the kids with the heaviest loads to carry. I wanted to model that kids with heavy loads need more love and support, not less.

Another benefit Covey points out is the impact on the 99 who are watching. When teachers saw me treating a struggling teacher in a fair manner it developed trust. When teachers and the other kids saw how I treated our most struggling students, it helped move the climate another degree towards caring about everyone in our community. Most teachers already leaned that direction, but this validated what they were doing and supported our community in being even more caring. How I treat people when they are struggling or have less power than me is also a mark of my personal character. Whether anyone else notices or cares isn't the point.

Several recent studies indicate that kids notice, too. Students who aren't in trouble fare better in schools with a collaborative approach to discipline. The "good kids" feel safer and can relax and learn without fearing that the teacher will lash out at them or treat them harshly if they screw up. Some of the studies even suggest that test scores are higher in schools with more collaborative and equitable approaches to teaching and discipline.

Covey's advice isn't just for educators. Clint found this to be true in the business world, too. Shortly after creating the Mosaic Company, an employee made an expensive and public mistake. Clint said most companies would have fired him immediately. Clint forgave him, asked him what he learned, and kept him on. This sent a message to Clint's team that mistakes are ok and it's ok to take a risk. He felt that the money lost was less important than the message sent, especially right as he was starting an innovative company. Here is how he describes his philosophy.

Clint

Mosaic also recognizes people are human and prone to make mistakes. But we always assume good intent. So, if our employees make a mistake, we'll be there to pick them up, dust them off, and help them move forward. Everyone fails. I have many times. We don't expect people to continue to make the same mistakes over and over, but in spite of this, we almost always give them another chance – it's how we learn. Since our employees feel safe, they don't operate from a place of fear regarding mistakes or bad decisions, knowing they won't lose their job or even their credibility when they fail. This frees our people to be innovative and be creative and take intelligent risks.

Showing grace isn't the same as having low expectations. This can be tricky at times and requires judgment. We set high expectations and challenge, even require, our team to be the best, and we reward excellence. And just like we don't expect people to be perfect, we aren't perfect at this either.

Steve

I agree that it is incredibly tricky balancing grace with high expectations. However, it can be done successfully most of the time. There were times it didn't work, but still felt like the right place to start, knowing we could change course if it wasn't working.

As Charlie Chaplin said, "You need power only when you want to do something harmful, otherwise love is enough to get things done."

This first year of my retirement, I haven't found my next sheep yet, but I'm looking. In the meantime, Cruz and I are having a ball. Even though he isn't "lost or struggling", I'm hoping our time together will benefit him.

Fred Astaire Syndrome

I hated dancing as a kid. Partly because I was a complete dork on the dance floor, and partly because I was always trying to look too cool to care about anything, especially girls. I wore the teenage look of, "I'm too cool to care about anything.", from about age six to 25. Rather than experiencing the arts, I hung out with the kids who chased the band, choir, and theater kids home at the end of the day. It would have been too high a cost to be seen with an artsy kid! Also, my church really frowned on dancing. Who knows what could happen at a dance, and what if the rapture came right when I was dancing? Would I have been left behind?

As an adult, it is one of my biggest regrets that I didn't sing, dance, or do theater earlier in my life. I was the lead role in that one play at Christian Heritage College and I loved that, but that was it. It was a comedy that reminded me of the "Get Smart" show on television. I made a great Maxwell. "Sorry about that, chief."

Millennials need to watch a few reruns of this show. It was hilarious. I still want to buy a shoe phone like Max used. I wonder if anyone sells those. I loved the laughter and applause of this theater experience. It reminded me of when I wanted to be a rock star!

I didn't realize how much I had missed out on until I became the principal at Roosevelt. The staff sang and danced for the kids at assemblies on a regular basis. The kids loved it, and I couldn't believe how much I enjoyed singing, dancing, and acting along with the team. When we all went through the training required to become an Arts Impact School, our staff of 30+ teachers spent three days acting, singing, painting, sculpting, and dancing together. A couple of years prior to this training, if you would have told me I would have to attend something like that, I would have figured out a way to be out of town or sick. By the time we had the training, I loved the arts.

Pablo Picasso stated, "Every child is an artist. The problem is how to remain an artist once we grow up."

The Arts Impact training impacted us as human beings, not just educators. We all wanted to be artists again. Teachers began attending plays, symphonies, operas, and concerts together. Fifteen years later, many of those same teachers are still painters, sing in choirs, act in community theater, write poetry or books. Our staff, parents, and kids all fell in love with the arts. There is a body of research about the power of the arts in schools, but you'll have to look that up yourself. This is my memoir and I'm too busy writing!

I took swing dance classes with Laketa about ten years ago, under the guise that everyone can learn to dance. After six lessons, I was just as bad as when I started. I felt sorry for my partner when we had to switch around. I hope they had strong shoes. Nonetheless, it was fun, and I've given myself permission to dance no matter how lousy I am. We're looking at doing line dance classes next. I think that even someone as nonrhythmic as I am could learn to march in a line and clap. I'll probably find out I'm wrong though.

Kids love dancing. I dance with Cruz all the time. When a salsa type music comes on the radio he yells, "Salsa, Papa." and away we go. When I'm home alone, I dance. I hummed and sang now and again in the office. That's not real popular. Try that one at your own risk.

At the Roosevelt weekly assemblies, we used to get all 600 kids and staff up to dance. We also had "dance drills". For a dance drill, I got on the intercom and explained how important all the drills were, like earthquake and fire drills. Then I asked the kids to stand by the side of their desks and listen carefully to the next instruction and immediately follow directions, just like in a fire drill. Their life could be at risk if they didn't master this drill! I would blast some 60's or 70's dance music and yell, "Dance"! I got a kick out of walking around the building while the song was playing and watching all the kids joyfully dancing. The teachers complained about the non-academic interruptions all the time, but I'm sure they secretly loved it. They danced right along with the kids.

After the song ended, I got back on the intercom and told the kids if anyone wasn't dancing to get their name to me. For the next week or two kids would run up giggling to tell me that someone in their class didn't dance. I'd tell them to warn that kid to watch his/her back. They raced off grinning to tell the kid, who usually wasn't too concerned. I used to love watching new kids when they came to our school, especially fourth and fifth grade boys. When we all got up to dance, they would stand around trying to look cool like I used to. After about three weeks, once they saw it was safe, they joined right in gleefully.

Two-year-old Cruz walked in the door yesterday, pointed at the tv and said, "Old Town Road, Papa. Old Town Road". We found the video and danced along with Lil Nas X and Billy Ray Cyrus. It's harder than it looks to get those cowboy steps down. Life is good.

21st Century Shakespeare

I looked at my program one more time to see if I had the right room. Every seat was filled and about a dozen people spilled into the hallway breathing over each other's shoulders. A confirmed germaphobe like Steve Morse was not going to be attending that session. My second choice had a similar crowd, so I kept looking. I was in New Orleans at an International Baccalaureate

Conference and somehow had overstayed my lunch break. Hard to believe, I know.

I finally found a session that was only about half-full, so I quickly darted in before the superintendent could see me wandering around in the hallway. I didn't want him to be sorry he had let me come with the team to New Orleans. I relaxed in my seat and opened my program to see what class I was attending. When I looked at the conference agenda, I realized I was now participating in a class on Spoken Word Poetry! Are you kidding! Torturous. It would be difficult to sneak out after coming in late and sitting in the front row where most of the open seats were. The presenters were young people with sincere smiles who welcomed me warmly, even asking my name. I didn't want to hurt their feelings, but I hadn't written a poem in fifty years and didn't consider myself a beatnik or poetry type person. I didn't even own a beret or a vest at the time.

The presenters turned out to be pretty doggone entertaining. I was thoroughly enjoying listening to their poems and digging the rap-like rhythm. (Or at least what a 55-year-old white male thinks rap rhythm sounds like.) This session turned out to be one of the best workshops I had attended in years. Near the end, we had an opportunity to write a first draft of several spoken word poems. I loved it and continued writing spoken word poems after returning home.

About a year after the conference, a friend gave me a workbook to practice writing skills. This got me into a wider range of poetry. As a school director, I had a captive audience of kids to try my poems out on and had a blast performing in classrooms around the district.

Every once in a while, I pour myself a cup of coffee, sit a spell, and write a poem or two. It's a great chance to reflect and discover something about myself. I'm glad I have finally discovered the arts. It's never too late. Here is one I enjoyed writing.

Water
Oftentimes my mind won't slow down,
Thoughts racing through me like a train in the middle of the night,
My life feels like a bobsled careening down the icy course,
Hugging the wall at 100 mph around the curves,
My mind spin round and round, but never getting anywhere,
Like a rider on a carousel, who returns to where he started,
Every sixty seconds, all day long,
Then I pull up a chair and gaze out at the bay.
I see the water, sometimes as smooth as glass,
Sometimes choppy with whitecaps leaping,
My pulse slows, my breathing deepens,
Water brings peace, grace to my soul
Stop, sit, look, listen to the waves slapping the shore,
The tide carries my worries out to sea.
Steve Morse 2016

Karen

Steve and Karen   *During chemo*

"Today you have two choices. We can either float down the Yakima River on innertubes or ride down Blewett Pass on your bikes.", said our sister Karen to Clint and me. I was about thirteen and Clint about eight at the time. Karen was the most fun sister in the world. We chose biking down Blewett Pass, Clint on his sting ray! This turned out to be the wrong choice, as there was a lot of traffic, we didn't have helmets and we probably reached speeds of fifty mph or higher. Clint flew over the front of his bike, losing his teeth and quite a bit of skin. Oh well, no complaints. Karen was the best.

If there were a contest for the best mom in America, I would have nominated Karen for that award, too. She loved her two boys intensely. She gave them 100 percent of herself every moment of every day. They both became successful adults and have wonderful children of their own. Every time I see them, I wish Karen were here. She would have been an incredible grandma.

Karen passed in the year 2000, after a battle with cancer. I miss her. I wish I would have mourned more at the time. I was still in my phase of denying any pain and putting on a smile. I always got stuck on the first step of denial and stayed there like a toddler looking up the staircase, afraid to take that second step.

My strategy left a lot of my soul behind. In the last ten years, I've allowed myself to dwell in pain, rather than instantly changing the subject. I have also spent more time remembering and mourning my sister, Karen. She was one of the most beautiful people in the world, inside and out. Every person she crossed paths with loved her. She cared about others and volunteered avidly.

After Karen passed, we realized that she was the glue holding our extended family together. We had a sibling weekend in the mountains last winter. We spent time remembering and missing her. We wrote a couple of poems.

Her final battle
A beautiful flower in the heat of the desert,
Blooming fully following a devastating thunderstorm,
That crushed everything else in its path,
Leaving a single flower in its wake,
Sadly, a desert flower departs quickly,
Why God?
We don't understand,

We were heartbroken,
As bone cancer ravaged her body,
Day by day,
But not without a fight,
What doctors said would be a month,
Extended a full year,
And not in bed,
A year of kicking, punching, biting that vile cancer,
Dodging and darting,
Smiling with a "f*** you" cancer smirk,
You ain't gonna stop me,

Departed for Europe with a smile and a prosthetic leg,
Rented a motorcycle in the south of France,
Fibbing to get Doug approved to drive,
Marched resolutely up staircase after staircase to see the castles,

Never complained or asked for help,
Sometimes Doug picked her up and carried her the last few steps
anyways,

Wasn't home long before departing on a road trip around the
country,
Slumbered peacefully leaning against the car door,
Waking every couple of hours,
to be thankful, filled with awe,
and to say, "I love you Doug",

Organized an extended family adventure,
Rambled the trails resolutely on one leg, smiling, pointing out
sites, happy,
We pretended to hear something behind us,
Turned around while we shed our tears,
She laughed, played table games, teased,
volunteered until the end,
Rocking crack babies, teaching immigrants to read,
Not a minute to squander her final year,
Despite the pain,

Yet at times,
Those who looked carefully,
Could see behind the smile,
There was an inner sadness,
A soul deeply wounded,
The ache of knowing that soon she would not be able to see her
kids and future grandkids,
An injury worse than losing a leg,

The cancer progressed,
She couldn't leave her bed,
Still smiled and held our hands when we dropped in,
Always grateful for company,
Glad to have one more opportunity to say, "I love you",
Teaching us to be better people,

Without saying a word,

Set a goal to greet the year 2000,
Battling, holding on like a gladiator,
Enduring the pain until 2 a.m., January 1, 2000,
Passed with Doug and Clint at her side,
Achieving her final goal,
Can't wait to see you again.
Steve, with help from Cheryl and Clint, June 2020

Karen
Sometimes I dream about you
I dream of finding you the perfect gift
I dream of diamonds and then I remember you never cared about these things
What can I give to you?
A day
A day like this:
Dawn breaks and you wake with two strong legs and thick, messy brown hair, no one cares if you comb it
Every person who loves you, who has been touched by you will be there today
Take our hands, we want to make you happy
You will spend this day free, totally free and smiling your biggest smile
On this day you ride bikes, even motorcycles, swim in the sun, ski in fresh snow, set up a tent, play soccer, go for hikes, finger paint, play cards, run with children, read books, and smell flowers
And still you make time to help someone
I will pick you up in my white convertible
We wear our shirts inside out just for a laugh
We drive away with the radio on, singing loudly with half the

words wrong
This is what I dream when I'm missing you
Laurel James 2020

Time to go home

The principal job can be demanding. I almost quit to do something else numerous times over the course of 24 years. After a few years at Roosevelt, I decided "Enough. It's time to go home." From that point on I made myself go home at a reasonable time, as I knew I would never get to the point where I was all done, and my kids would be gone before I knew it. Because I seemed to be an effective principal without working a bazillion hours, other principals often asked me how I made that happen. One of the assistant superintendents also told principals to meet with me to get tips on prioritization and working a more reasonable number of hours.

Most principals I met with wanted specific strategies or tools and charts. I didn't really have any. I had only two pieces of advice. 1) Identify core values. Spend time on the most important tasks, and almost none on the rest. 2) Decide to go home at a certain time and stick to it. That wasn't a satisfying answer to most people I met with. They wanted lists and strategies.

I concur with Shauna Niequist in her book entitled, "Present over Perfect", when she wrote, "I first thought changes were needed in time management, but realized I needed to remake myself from the inside out."

While implementing a few tips would have been easier than remaking myself, I have seldom seen anyone make significant dents in reducing time at work without a paradigm shift about what is important in their job and life. I made a commitment to myself and my family to leave at a designated time. Once I made that promise, I could honestly let people know that was I unavailable due to another commitment.

Nanea Hoffman learned, "Instead of focusing so much on a to do list, I'm starting a to be list. Things I want to be: Happy, Calm, Loving, Healthy, Awesome."

I saw the light

I was standing in the living room one afternoon talking with Laketa, when suddenly, I could tell I was going down for the count. Luckily, the couch was right behind me and I flopped safely backwards. I entered a dream-like state where I relived almost my entire life. I thought I had died because the memories were in order and played out in real time. It was comparable to being in a movie theater and seeing all the major events of my life. Probably wouldn't have won an Oscar, as my life isn't all that exciting, but personally I gave it five stars. It brought back lots of great memories.

When I came to, I thought I had been out for days and expected to see my family huddled around me wondering when I was going to come out of this coma. The movie seemed at least that long, another reason it probably wouldn't win an Oscar. I could remember specific details about major life occurrences. I felt dazed and confused, as if I had been spinning around in a time machine and deposited on the couch. I was so exhausted that I felt like I had run a marathon while fighting the flu. I couldn't believe I was still on the couch. Had Laketa just left me there and gone about her daily life, back and forth to work, eating meals? I would never do that to her!

I asked Laketa how long I had been out, and she said I had only been out for about thirty seconds. That didn't seem even remotely possible, but Laketa's extremely honest, so I believed it. We called the doctor and after ascertaining that I was fine, he told me that it was probably a TIA and if it happened again, I would need to come in for an appointment. That seemed like less concern than I was expecting. I didn't even have to come to the office. How about a little empathy, doc? I thought I'd died, and he acted like it was no big deal. However, like most people, I hated going to the doctor so that answer was fine with me.

If you haven't experienced a TIA, you are really missing out. A transient ischemic attack (TIA) is a brief interruption to blood flow to the part of the brain that causes temporary stroke-like symptoms. It was an incredible experience and made me wonder if hallucinogens might be similar. I was always terrified of drugs, which turned out not to be such a bad thing, but this made we wonder what I had missed out on. I debated if I should start for a few minutes, but as an elementary school principal and the father of two young children I decided to wait. Also, I'm kind of afraid of needles, and since I made it to age 64 without a major addiction, I decided to stay the course for the time being. If you are reading this and get hooked on cocaine, the author takes no responsibility. I don't know if it will be anything like my TIA. I do know though; Einstein's theories about space and time seem much more believable following this event. I lived hundreds of hours in just a few seconds. Our experience of time is an enigma.

It never happened again and for a few days I felt much wiser and more content. The sky was bluer, the grass was greener, the Pop Tarts tasted sweeter. Of course, my wisdom and new perspective didn't last. Nothing is ever quite that easy in life.

Another time, I was playing on the banks of the Salmon-La-Sac River at about age eight. The river was high, and my dad came by to warn Ralph and me to be extremely cautious. If we fell in, we would be swept downstream, hit our head on a big rock and drown. I gave this advice the same consideration that I gave all parental admonishment at the time and ignored it the moment he walked away. I suppose parents in the 21st Century might be more hands on and make the kid move to another spot or stop playing a couple of feet from the slippery banks of a dangerous river, but in those days that was darn good parenting. I'm sure Dad felt he had done his duty and returned to the campfire.

Mom was probably the one who made him walk over and tell us in the first place. He could relax again.

Sure enough, about five minutes later, I slipped and fell into the river. I thrashed and grabbed at anything I could get my hands on. Somehow, I grabbed a root wad and hung on for dear life while Ralph went running and yelling towards the campsite. His older brother heard and pulled me out of the river. This was not the same brother who practiced his torture techniques on us. During the minute or so I was in the water, I was sure I was going to die. Once again, I was exceptionally wise for a couple of hours, at least by third grade standards of wisdom, and then back to normal. Almost getting in a car accident has the same impact on me. I slow down and am very thankful for a while and then forget in a few days.

Interestingly, when I thought I was going to die, or thought I actually had died, a peace settled over me, even as I scrabbled to hang on to the roots in the freezing water. I have read books about how much people changed after a near death experience, but these experiences didn't do much for me. Maybe they weren't near enough to death. Or maybe I'm just the kind of dude who doesn't really learn much even when whacked upside the head or shot in the eye. Or, maybe growth is more incremental, and few people make significant life changes after a scare. One day at a time, I guess.

Deal me in

Snow was falling on the deck outside the sliding glass door. I was holding two Aces in my hand when Drew called "all-in". We still hadn't seen the flop. I folded.

I played a little poker with Joel and his pals when they were in high school, especially over Winter Break when none of us had school. I tended to play it safe and could hang in the game for a long time. I often finished in the money as a top three player.

However, I rarely took the top prize money home. I had to overcome my fear of going all in. With practice, I learned when to put it all on the line. It always made me nervous, but I trained my rational brain to overcome my feeling brain to go "all in" when the time came. You had to be patient and wait for the right time, but when the time was right you had to take the risk. Those who let the feeling part of the brain overcome the rational part and went "all in" too frequently, seldom lasted long in our games, or on tv.

Joel watched poker tournaments on tv. I've never watched them alone, but I enjoyed watching it with him. I was interested in how and when they chose to go "all in", as that was so applicable to my job and life. As a principal, I had to learn when to go "all in" and leave it all on the table for high impact initiatives.

General McArthur said, "It is fatal to enter any war without the will to win it." Once I chose to go "all in", I dug in and fought to hold that hill.

I had a lot of fun playing poker with the gang, and I haven't become a gambling addict yet! Don't believe Laketa, Lianne, Hal, Dana, and the others who tell you that they think I'm addicted. I know my limit and play within it.

Also, don't blame me if you become addicted and go bankrupt. You're an adult. (At least I hope you are. There are much better children's books from which to choose. I may need to speak with your parents, young person!) As a semi-functional adult, you are responsible for your own choices. However, you will also need to add the skill of knowing when to fold.

Knowing when to fold was the only way I survived as a principal. If everything was important then nothing was important. The educators I observed who were struggling the most made every issue into a battle. Folding on non-priority topics saved my skin.

I recognize that there are lots of worthwhile initiatives in education and life. There are many ways to skin a cat! However, the question I asked was, "Why would we want to skin this cat in the first place?" Are we required to skin every cat that skitters across our path? Let's just leave that cat alone for the time being. That cat's not a priority right now.

With challenging students, I took a similar approach and worked on one behavior at a time and folded on some of the lesser priority behaviors. Until kids have a couple of basic compliance skills, the other skills are pipe dreams. Same with Joel and Lianne. We let their rooms look like toxic waste dumps eventually, rather than continuing to fight about cleaning their rooms. I would never have successfully negotiated the myriad of relationships at work (or home!) without knowing when to fold.

You'll never believe this, but when I was a senior in high school, I was kind of a smart mouth. I rarely backed down from a verbal altercation. I was never in a fistfight, but no one got the best of me in a verbal exchange. One night after tennis practice, I was one of two people left in the locker room. The other guy threw shotput on the track team and was strong as an ox. The coach dropped two towels on the bench and announced he was leaving. He asked us to double check that the door slammed locked behind us when we left. What a different world. No coach would ever leave a couple of kids behind now!

After the coach left, Hans informed me in no uncertain terms that both those towels were his. When I asked how I was supposed to dry off, he suggested maybe the paper towel dispenser would work, following a statement letting me know that it wasn't his f***ing problem. His level of concern didn't seem quite as high as my level of concern.

He had a full cast on one leg at the time, so this seemed more like a verbal than physical battle. It seemed very winnable. As I got out of the shower, I picked up one of the towels and said, "I don't think you can catch me with that cast on. I'm pretty quick." I broke into a huge grin, thinking I had him right where I wanted him. Bahahaha.

He pondered a few seconds before replying, "I might not catch you today." He turned around in the shower seemingly unconcerned. Hmm... In just six words, he shifted the equation. I reconsidered my decision for about ten more seconds before tossing him the towel. To this day, when I choose to walk away from a battle, I remember heading for the paper towel dispenser in the Auburn High locker room.

That's all I have to say about this for now, so I'm going to fold, and wait for a better hand.

What a Wonderful World

Walking through the halls at Roosevelt on a rainy winter day I was feeling kind of blue. It seemed there was always one more problem. I started to feel like the world is kind of a lousy place. Why should the kids get kicked in the teeth all the time? Even if they end up a mess as adults, can't they have a good childhood at least? Suddenly I heard, "It's a Wonderful World", playing in one of the kindergarten classrooms.

I stepped into the classroom, sat on one of those tiny kindergarten chairs, and just watched the kids and listened to the music. I found tears coming to my eyes as I heard 25 little voices singing that song while playing/working together. For the length of that song, in that one classroom in Bellingham, Washington, the world was a wonderful world full of kids of all races and socioeconomic classes singing and working together.

Many situations in our world appear completely messed up. Poverty, injustice, extreme global and national disparity of wealth and health, oppression, and war. It doesn't seem like the right way to run a planet. For those who believe in God, me included, it doesn't seem as if our current state is what He or She hoped for. Wasn't the world supposed to turn out differently?

However, when I keep my eyes and ears open, I often see slices here and there of a wonderful world. When I catch a glimpse, I try to pause and celebrate the moment.

The other night when I was having an honest and open conversation about race with an African American friend. I saw our reflection in the restaurant window and paused and thought, "This is the way the world is supposed to work. These are the kinds of conversations people are supposed to have." Even if only for a moment, it was worth celebrating.

We get glimpses all the time if we are mindful. I saw it regularly at Roosevelt. I paused when I saw...

- a lunch table with Latino, African American, White, and Native kids chattering away
- a kindergarten girl hugging and comforting a crying kindergarten boy
- teachers collecting money for kids and families, even when those same kids/families wore us out with behaviors and complaints
- when a teacher who had been at our school for over 25 years and was retiring in a year volunteered to move to another school and spend her last year among strangers, so a beginning teacher could stay at Roosevelt. That new teacher is still at Roosevelt almost 20 years later.

In my personal life, I try to pause and recognize when a neighbor says "hey", when another driver waves me in, when someone smiles at me. Going places with Cruz has tripled the amount of times I see this. People wave, smile and want to talk to us. Cruz smiles and responds. Sometimes, if I'm doing most of the talking with a neighbor, he says, "Cruz turn, Papa". When I say, "What do you want to tell them, Cruz?"

He says, "Monster trucks."

We pause and let him tell us all the names of Monster Trucks he knows. That's a wonderful world. If we are at the playground, Cruz might just start chasing and playing with other kids with no introduction necessary. Kids have an openness and friendliness about them that allows interaction quickly.

I have attempted to cultivate my childlike friendliness. If I see someone I want to play with, I probably won't chase them, but I'll ask them if they want to play. I drove by a tennis court on my way home from work every night for 21 years. I typically glanced over hoping to find a new player. One summer, I noticed a group that had been there several evenings in a row. I stopped and introduced myself. They sent me home with instructions to change clothes and come back with my racquet immediately. I ended up playing with this group several nights a week for a couple of summers before we moved.

They were a group of refugees from Vietnam, so I also learned a few Vietnamese phrases and heard lots of interesting stories of their homeland. I got way more than playing tennis out of the deal. Lest you think I had nothing to offer them; I was able to teach them several swear words, a few folksy sayings like, "Don't let the door hit you on the way out." "Don't cry over spilled milk." "D'oh." and "Don't be a schmuck". I made them laugh a lot with hand gestures and guttural yells when I made dumb mistakes and loved hearing them yell, "D'oh" when they missed an easy shot.

We laughed and had a great time and they got after me if I missed a few days in a row, so I figured I must be welcome. I was at least ten years older than they were and when I stumbled or fell, I would hear rapid fire Vietnamese and howling laughter. When I asked if they were laughing at me, they smiled broadly, winked, and said "Of course not." Those warm summer evenings of laughing and playing with people from halfway around the globe felt like a wonderful world.

As I write tonight, we are mid-pandemic with high unemployment rates and social unrest. It's difficult not to get discouraged. However, I just got a text from Lianne. As she was tucking Cruz into bed, he told her that he wants to have a puppet show with me tomorrow. I can't wait. The world *is* still "wonderful."

Mirror, mirror on the wall

Striding confidently down the Roosevelt hallway in my blue hair, a kid walked by and said, "Cool hair, Mr. M." I thanked him and asked if he liked it better when it was brown or the blue style that I had died it for a school fundraiser. He got a funny look on his face and the teachers listening in started grinning. They chipped in, "Brown? Wishful thinking."

I asked Laketa that evening if she would describe my hair as "mostly gray or mostly brown". She cracked up and said it had been almost all gray for some time.

I seldom look in a mirror and almost never very closely. While reflecting about my life experiences has been helpful, I have found the opposite to be true when it comes to looking in a mirror at my physical self. I am generally more satisfied with my looks and physique the less often I look. In my mind, I still look about 35.

I showed up at work one morning and several people said they really liked my hair that day. They asked if I got a haircut or was doing something differently. Turns out, it was a warm day and

I had driven to work with wet hair and the car windows open. I guess my hair looked better when the wind messed it all up. Ugh. Maybe I should have used a mirror more often.

Nonetheless, this strategy has been better than exercise for giving me a healthy body-image. I'll never understand why anyone would buy those magnifying mirrors that show every tiny fault. What's up with that? With a quick glance, I can usually think, "Dang. I still look pretty doggone good. You da' man, Steve."

The day after spring break about ten years ago, a teacher announced that she had a story that summed up the main difference between men and women. Our ears perked up. This would either be a fascinating anecdote, or we would be able to report her to HR for an inappropriate comment. Either way, it was worth listening carefully to.

She had been in Hawaii with her husband for their 25th anniversary. They were putting on their swimsuits to head to the beach. After looking in the full-length mirror, she thought, "Ugh. I look nothing like I did 25 years ago. I'll buy a coverup downstairs in the lobby."

When she moved aside, her husband stepped forward, looked in the same mirror, vigorously shook his beer belly and announced, "Damn. I still look pretty fine after 25 years." We cracked up. If you can't avoid mirrors, at least interpret what you see positively!

As for me, it's been easier to avoid mirrors since retiring. However, once in a while, Laketa makes me shave or comb my hair and it slows my strut for a few days.

THE FINAL LAP AROUND THE SCHOOL YARD ... 2014-2019

New pair of glasses

Laketa and I visited Hurricane Ridge on the Olympic Peninsula last July. We drove nineteen miles up a steep windy road through a magnificent forest to arrive at the ridge. From the top, we had a significantly different perspective about where we were staying in Port Angeles. We could observe the whole picture, not just the street directly in front of the house. It's crucial to step out of the fray and get on the ridge (or even a balcony) and look at the whole picture now and again.

We stood at the base of the lodge and admired the view from every angle. It was about fifteen degrees colder up there, so I went into the lodge after a while. I climbed the stairs and looked at the view from the window upstairs. It was only about ten feet higher, but the view and my perspective shifted yet again. The ridge is 5,242 feet above sea level, so ten more feet was much less than a one percent shift in my perspective but changed the view again.

We then walked about four blocks to view the other side of the ridge and had a **completely** different view in a four-block walk. We didn't need to drive another nineteen miles to see a landscape vastly different. This trip reminded me that looking at things from even a slightly different perspective can make a difference.

"When we change the way we look at things. The things we look at change." Dr. Wayne Dyer

One other interesting note is that our Subaru (This is not a paid advertisement!) averaged six miles per gallon on the way up the ridge and 97.9 MPG on the way down, ... a personal record! That's generally what happens when we begin to shift our perspective. It can be a grind at first, but when you or your team really hits the flow, it can feel as if you are extremely efficient!

Changing perspective has been a step by step process for me for most of my life, but about the time I turned fifty, my ability to see situations from a different viewpoint grew exponentially. I felt like someone had handed me a new pair of magic glasses. I began perceiving the world differently, both personally and at work.

In Fredrik Backman's book, *my grandmother asked me to tell you she's sorry*, the grandma tells her granddaughter that when a person enters heaven, they are given a new pair of glasses. These glasses allow the wearer to see situations and other people differently. I'm experiencing a little of that right now and hope that grandma is right about the next world. I have a long way to go, but I feel like I'm on the right path.

"To acquire knowledge, one must study; To acquire wisdom, one must observe." Marilyn vos Savant

Cancer didn't turn me into The Buddha, but there were a few benefits

We were finishing our family supper when the phone rang with an unknown number. I almost let it ring, but something told me to answer. It was my doctor. This seemed like an unusual time to call. He informed me that I had prostate cancer. A tear ran down my cheek and an immense weight of sadness immediately overwhelmed me. It was surreal how my whole body felt differently in a heartbeat. My legs felt too heavy to walk.

I listened to him silently for a minute or two. When he asked if I had any questions, I was too numb to think of a single question. We hung up a moment later in what now seems like the shortest cancer telephone call in history.

After quietly crying for three or four minutes, my reaction shifted to my go-to strategy of denial and putting on a happy face. I began thinking and verbalizing, "I've had a surprisingly good run. Yes, 55 is a bit young, but I've had a great life so far." It was years before I allowed myself to mourn my loss.

I was determined to fight the cancer. Due to the aggressive nature of my diagnosis, I ended up doing surgery, radiation, and hormone therapy. The treatments totally sucked. I won't go into detail on all of them, but I have one story that kind of sums up what a pain in the ass the whole thing was.

As it turns out, a catheter can get clogged. I wasn't aware of that, were you? And guess what? The doctor doesn't want to hear about it and won't help you when that happens! I called on a Saturday morning and informed the doctor that my catheter was no longer draining.

He calmly replied, "No problem. This happens quite often. All you have to do is twist it around 360 degrees several times and it will unclog."

I almost fainted. It's like being told that all you need to do is urinate on an electric fence for thirty seconds and everything will be fine.

I replied, "I can't possibly do that. You have no idea how skittish I am. You are going to have to make an exception and meet me in the office" I was sure he must occasionally make exceptions for people like myself. I made exceptions for kids at school when it seemed like the right thing to do!

"I'm not willing to meet you. I've been doing this for thirty years and I have to be firm, or I would be doing this several times every weekend. You'll just have to do it."

Unbelievable. I knew I wouldn't be able to make myself do this and assumed I'd end up in the ER in a few days with toxic shock syndrome or something caused by urine buildup. Luckily, I had a plan B. Laketa was a certificated medical assistant. I've seen the license! She gave shots, drew blood, and did all kinds of stuff to people. I'll just ask her, close my eyes, and block my mind.

When I asked her, she thought about it for about 1/10 of a second before replying, "I'm not doing that. Good luck. I'm sending good thoughts your way."

Now what was I supposed to do. Everyone knows how skittish I am. I mentally brainstormed how I could set up a rope and tie the catheter to a rock and throw it out the upstairs window and other wacky inventions. After figuring that could turn out a lot worse than just twisting it, I gritted my teeth and got ready. It reminded me of the times I jumped off a bridge into the Green River in high school. I typically counted to three without jumping at least five or six times before I jumped. This was the same. After five or six times counting, I did it!

(Apparently, my dad's question, "If your friends jumped off a bridge would you jump off a bridge?", didn't really take.)

Aye caramba!!!!! For about ten seconds the pain was excruciating, and I let out a scream. It worked though, and I felt the same manliness I experienced jumping off bridges into rivers, running outside with no shirt in below zero weather, etc.

I wanted everyone to be as excited as I was, but my family just said, "Oh, that's good." They were apparently too busy getting ready to go to Joel's college graduation. Big deal. Twisting that catheter was way harder than getting a college degree.

I spent the next five days checking my catheter about every minute or two to see if it was clogged again. My experience went from ... "This is the life. It doesn't get much better than this. I can snack and watch tv all day and not even have to get up to go to the bathroom.", to ..." I'm terrified I will have to do that again. Now that I realize how much it hurts; I hope I never have to go through that again if I live to be 200 years old." It was kind of a mood killer.

I've heard that most men will get prostate cancer if they live long enough. My advice to any men taking notes is to wait until you are much older than 55 to get it. I also recommend you quit taking notes and just try to enjoy reading the book.

Most people seem to believe that cancer survivors have incredible wisdom available only to those who have stared down the beast. It definitely granted me insight, but I didn't gain the great wisdom that anyone would climb a mountain to sit at my feet and hear about. I was surprised that I still seemed like pretty much the same guy.

It wasn't a lightning flash of inspiration. I didn't want to hike the Appalachian Trail or go sky diving. Although, I did let my daughter talk me into sky diving with her once. That wasn't as fun as I thought it would be. The spinning around on the final descent almost made me puke.

Nonetheless, I did gain some inner wisdom and developed a slightly different perspective on life. Cancer assisted me in realigning my priorities, it made the grass a little greener, and it created more intimate relationships. I began to express my emotions more, was a bit more thankful, and maybe slightly wiser.

Clint told me that recovery was like that for him. It turned out to be mostly just a lot of hard work, and not a lightning flash of inspiration. He didn't feel like a totally different person when he finished either. He was clean and able to leave his obsessive thoughts behind but was still himself. He said many of the guys he met in recovery felt similarly.

There were several awesome side benefits. I felt unconditionally loved by many people. Lianne came over every night after work and plopped on the corner of the bed with her phone and laptop and just hung out with me for a few hours. She showed her care by her presence. She asked if I needed food or water every fifteen minutes or so. I usually did. Joel also came by regularly. He popped in, said "hey", and left after half an hour, but I knew he cared. Laketa was patient and kind, and the teachers from Roosevelt signed up and a teacher or two came a couple of nights a week for five- or six-weeks bearing food. I was moved to tears almost every day. The month I spent recovering from cancer surgery is still one of my favorite months.

I sat on the couch and played computer games and binge-watched multiple tv series. My nephew brought me a couple seasons of "Curb Your Enthusiasm" with Larry David. We had never seen that show before and howled so hard we almost fell off the couch several times.

Author's Warning ... If you ever get prostrate surgery, I recommend not laughing too heartily before you get your catheter out.

Nonetheless, I am more thankful for everything in my life and every day that I'm on this earth, a wee bit wiser, and I feel more loved than pre-cancer, at least when I take the time to be mindful of it.

It reminds me of the Charlie Brown comic where Charlie says, "One day you will die, Snoopy., and Snoopy replies, "Yes, but every other day we will live."

If you are looking for any other Buddha-like wisdom from me, you'll be disappointed. However, here's a poem I wrote following my treatments.

Cancer
Cancer climbed my fence last night,
Like a thief, smashed his way through the window of my soul,
Unexpectedly, while I was doing something else,
Uninvited, unwelcome, he did not enter gently,
Who is he to be so bold? He was not supposed to be in my yard,
I did not plan for this. I don't have time,
Why me?......
The surgeon's knife cuts deep. The medications dull my senses,
Woozy, I stay in bed, even my thinking slow.

But I am astonished, surprised,
Is it possible that hard is not always bad?
That pain can be a mentor,
That friends and family love me more than I thought?

That sunsets are suddenly more vivid,
The birds are coming to our deck more often,
The grass is greener, the sky bluer?

My wife is at my side, ensuring that I take care of myself,
Her love like a glove on my hand,
My daughter stops every evening, just to be with me,
The world is still spinning,
The sun comes up every morning,
The tide goes in and out,

Cancer, like a robber, took something from me,
But also left a gift behind,
New eyes, a new heart
The value of time exponentially increasing, like smoke rising from a chimney.
Steve Morse 2012

Clueless White Guy from NW Washington State

The 2020 Black Lives Matter protests feel like an alarm clock that we have been pressing snooze on for way too long. I was always aware that our country, and specifically our educational system, had some substantial equity issues to solve. Schools have been doing reasonably well with middle and upper-class white kids, but still have significant disparities for students in poverty, students with disabilities, and minority populations. This is a complicated issue that isn't easy to solve. It's definitely a larger societal issue and not just a school issue, but I could only control what I did at school, so I focused on that aspect.

My personal alarm clock ripped me right out of bed in 2014 when I accepted the job as Civil Rights Director for the district. After 34 years in the public schools, I discovered that I was still at a beginning level in my understanding of the degree of systemic racism in our society and how the schools and the government were complicit. I had a very rudimentary understanding of redlining, sunset laws, and how the inequalities were perpetuated by the government. I'd assumed it was mostly a few bad individuals and didn't realize how deeply it was cooked into the system. I also didn't understand my own complicity.

This really blew a hole in my mind and I found myself thinking, "How did I live 55 years on planet earth without understanding more about this stuff." I don't remember being taught much, if anything, about some of the history of how we got to where we are. I'm still nowhere close to an expert and have a ton to learn.

It looks as if I might not be taking this expedition in isolation. My sibs and I have been talking about this quite a bit the last couple of weeks, and it seems like people around the world are delving more deeply into systemic racism currently, due to the George Floyd protests.

Richard Rohr has written some excellent daily reflections on racism in the last several weeks. Here is one he wrote this week that really resonated with my experience. "The Second Conversion to solidarity is anger at the unjust situation that caused their poverty. Many people never reach this stage of anger at injustice, especially in the United States. Our cultural worship of individualism and "bootstrap" mentality deprives us of the capacity to empathize with people in need and recognize systemic oppression. When we are in the middle or upper tier of privilege, it is almost impossible to see the many ways the system helped us succeed. We have to pay attention to whomever is saying "I can't breathe" to recognize the biases at work. ... This often only changes when, through friendship with people of different backgrounds and life experiences, we witness mistreatment and marginalization. We get to know someone outside our immediate social circle. "– Richard Rohr

Richard hit the nail on the head for me. I had been reading, attending conferences, and meeting with marginalized groups in my new role as the district Civil Rights Officer, but developing a close personal relationship with an African American administrator made the learning me to life.

Having someone who I could talk openly and honestly with about his past and present experiences with race during this time of learning was powerful. In my experience, I rarely shift my opinions just by reading/studying. My learning style is definitely relational. It reminds me of the senators and pastors who were voting and speaking against gay rights but changed their minds when their own child came out as LGBTQ. Relationships change our thinking more powerfully than books.

My friend's name is Q and we could both tell we were going to be buddies about five minutes after we met. It was one of those times in my life where I felt like I clicked with someone immediately. He said he felt the same way. He asked me to be his mentor, and I ended up getting the better deal from the mentorship. He gave me a new pair of glasses that helped me see things from a different angle. He helped me challenge my assumptions gently, but consistently. He was able to subtly, and at times not so subtly, shift my perspective without ever once seeming preachy or judgmental. Q treated me like a brother and made me feel comfortable enough to talk through the tough issues around race. We also had a similar sense of humor and teased each other relentlessly, so the relationship wasn't like some intense counseling session or anything. Even the hardest conversations were punctuated with laughter and felt natural.

We had the opportunity to spend four days together in New Orleans attending the National Association of Black School Educators Conference a few years ago. This was an incredible opportunity to immerse myself in an experience outside my comfort zone, look at issues from a different perspective, and to quietly listen and learn from others. I usually talk way too much, but it was easy for me to close my big mouth there. Even I'm not naïve enough to share my limited expertise and insight on racial problems to a 99 percent black audience. I wish I had attended this type of conference thirty years earlier. It would have been extremely helpful in my work. Although, I may not have been as ready for the learning at that time. Life has a way of teaching us when we are ready.

When Q invited me to go with him, I was a little nervous and asked him if I'd be the only white guy. He let out his booming laugh and said "Don't worry about that. I've got your back." That didn't really answer my question, but I swallowed a lump in my throat and consented to the trip. The fact that the conference was in New Orleans didn't hurt! Also, Q is a great eater and

I knew we would eat our way through that whole town given four days to complete the task.

About five minutes after the trip was booked, I started worrying again about Q's, "Don't worry.", response. Would I be the only white guy there? He dodged that question well. I could just imagine disembarking from the plane in Louisiana and Q saying, "By the way, you will be the only white guy here." and laughing his head off. He would get a kick out of retelling that story for the rest of his life.

So, I called the organization headquarters in DC and the guy on the phone reassured me that allies were welcome and there were always a few white people there. He probably thought I was just another clueless white guy from Washington State.

All my fears turned out to be completely unfounded. Everyone was so friendly and helpful. And, for the record, there were about a dozen other white people there out of the 800 attendees. Nobody seemed to even give it a second thought.

That didn't stop Q from teasing me though. He went out of his way to look for opportunities to chuckle at me for stuff I didn't know, or to ask, "I would be interested in what the white guy thinks?", to embarrass me in front of dozens of people in a breakout group. He teased me all week and videotaped taped me when I tried to mumble along to the Black National Anthem. I didn't even realize there was a black national anthem and I wasn't going to kneel or stand there without opening my mouth!

The first event I signed up for was a bus tour of the city. Q signed up for a class about tips for becoming an effective black superintendent. I was a long shot to land a job as a black superintendent, so I didn't join him for that session. I arrived at the bus a few minutes late and the bus was waiting. The only open seat was in the back, so I got a taste of how Q feels every day in lily white Bellingham. I walked my butt down the aisle bumping into people and saying "excuse me" every five seconds. I plopped down warily. Within seconds, the lady next to me and the people around me introduced themselves and greeted me warmly. I gave a sigh of relief and had the same experience in every session I entered for the next four days.

This conference ended up being lifechanging. I'm kind of embarrassed now that I was nervous about going. I wasn't scared that people would be mean or treat me badly, I just didn't want to look like an interloper. I didn't want to be in anyone else's way or keep people from speaking freely. I just wanted to go to learn. Anyways, I hope I learn as much about racial issues in the next five years as I learned in the last five. It would be great to be at least a little bit less clueless.

Grade yourself on a curve (and in some areas, pass/fail)
Laketa and I were heading to a movie with Clint and his wife, Shelly. Clint and I were talking about some of the stupid things people had recently done that we had read about or seen on tv. We were patting ourselves on the back for not being as idiotic as some of the celebrities and knuckleheads out there.

Shelly, who finishes regularly in the top ten for calling out BS, asked us why we always compared ourselves favorably to idiots, rather than comparing ourselves to people we could aspire to be. She thought that maybe we had the wrong approach. Laketa, of course, quickly agreed and jumped on board.

Clint and I looked at each other and thought, "Why on earth would we ever do that? We have enough negative messaging in our heads from our childhood. We spend our days acting tough and cocky, while underneath the bravado we have terrible self-images. No, thanks, Shelly. We're going to continue comparing ourselves to the worst people we can find. That way we can proudly proclaim, 'At least we aren't serial killers, gang members, or arrogant celebrities falling through windows at parties.'

We think this is a great strategy.".

This strategy has served me reasonably well over the years. Perfectionism is probably one of the leading causes of the anxiety kids are experiencing today. I'm sure it contributes to adult anxiety, also.

A Roosevelt teacher gave me a book entitled, "The Underachiever's Manifest. The Guide to Accomplishing Little and Feeling Great.", by Ray Bennett, M.D. She gave me this as a practical joke, thinking I wouldn't read it. I grinned, looked through the chapter headings, and tossed it in a drawer, figuring she was right and that I probably wouldn't ever read it.

A couple of years later, I was looking for something I needed in the drawer and spotted the book. I started reading and couldn't put it down. I finished the book in about 20-30 minutes. This turned out to be one of the most profound little books I have ever read. Our society today puts so much pressure on people to be the best at everything. The author showed the benefits of slowing down and being ok with being average at most things. It was hilarious and a reminder to go easy on myself. I needed to prioritize which things to try to be the best at, while allowing myself to be graded on a curve or pass/fail on most things.

"Hype", by Dr. Nina Shapiro, explores similar concepts around health issues. You can be healthy without doing everything to the max. You can talk a walk and don't have to do a marathon. You can drink a reasonable amount of tap water and don't need to drink twelve servings of a special water every day, etc.

Fortunately for me, I had a head start on this lesson. I learned to grade myself on a curve from about age five on. When mom or the teacher would ask me why I did something, I answered by letting them know that at least it wasn't as bad as something that someone else had done! It never got me out of trouble and I had to hear the speech entitled, "If your friend jumped off a bridge would you.", about 10,000 times, but at least I knew in my own heart that I wasn't as crummy as that other kid. That helped me sleep soundly at night.

Grading myself on a curve and comparing myself primarily to the bottom ten percent has allowed me to accomplish many things in life that I might never have attempted. It allowed me to fake it till I made it. In a lot of areas, I grade myself pass/fail in order to spend my time and energy on more important issues like becoming a better dad, spouse, principal, etc. Here is a partial list of things I never would have attempted without buoying my self-image with comparisons to the bottom ten percent.

- tell an interview committee what a great teacher or principal I would become by comparing myself to my worst teachers, leading to actual jobs
- give my first speech
- lead my first workshop
- ask Laketa to marry me
- become a parent (I was able to convince myself I would be a much better parent than the parents who hit and yell at their kids 24/7!)
- try new sports and activities
  write and share my first poem
- write this book

Clint, would you please let Shelly know that after reflecting on this issue again many years later, I'm going to continue not comparing myself to world class runners, professional athletes, Mother Teresa, etc. It's worked out great so far.

Sometimes all you need is a mom

I was beginning to get a headache. I had been in my office with a five-year old kid who had been screaming at the top of his lungs and tipping over furniture for about three hours. District protocol was to never physically restrain a child unless they were hurting themselves or others. Even on long days like this, I appreciated that policy. I never wanted to wrestle around with some kid, and I really didn't want to get bit. I was waiting him out and tying my best to project an aura of calmness in the room. I usually only tried to wait kids out for about half an hour before getting a parent in, but we couldn't get hold of Jake's mom. Luckily, his daycare was about forty yards away, right across the field. We could see it!

The daycare owner said she couldn't walk over to get him, as she had a baby and several toddlers, but she offered to step out her door and wave him over. All we needed to do was walk Jake about thirty feet from the office where he could see her and run over. We couldn't get Jake to stand up or even walk out the door of my office though.

Jake started getting more violent. I only involved the police a couple of times in my 25 years as a principal, but I thought this might be a good time to call. Good grief, we only needed to move him about ten yards. I hoped Jake would be excited to walk outside to see the police car.

The officer arrived in my office about 45 minutes later. A five-year old throwing a tantrum definitely isn't a code red. His presence had absolutely zero impact and Jake continued his tantrum unabated. Jake was slightly calmer when ignored, so the officer and I chit chatted at the conference table for about twenty minutes. We were now approaching four hours of his tantrum, which didn't seem healthy for Jake and seemed totally unnecessary when we could see his daycare right through my window. I asked the officer if he could just gently lead him by the arm to the door and let him run across the field. The officer was about 6'5" and looked like an ex professional football player.

"No way," he said immediately. "I'm not getting accused of excessive force. Why don't you do it?"

I chuckled and said the exact same thing back to him, word for word. As a male principal, I didn't want to be on a social media video dragging a screaming and kicking five-year old kid out of the school.

After another ten minutes or so, the secretary couldn't handle the yelling another minute. JoLynda walked in, grabbed Jake by the hand and stated, "Come on. We're leaving.", grabbed his hand and walked him across the street.

The officer and I stared at each other a minute or two thinking, "What the hell? That was easy." Then we started laughing. Here sat two highly trained professionals. We both had specific de-escalation training, and I allegedly was an expert on how to deescalate young children. I could have wallpapered the wall with my early childhood certificates. Jake didn't seem to need two certificated experts though. All he needed was "a mom" to walk in, grab his hand, and say, "Come on. We're going across the street." JoLynda had two boys at home and always approached the kids at school about like she approached her boys at home.

A neighbor mom taught me to swim when I was eight years old, not a certificated swim teacher. She was a high school PE teacher. I was the only kid watching, rather than swimming, in her backyard pool. She asked me why I wasn't swimming and when I told her I didn't know how to swim; she picked me up, threw me in and talked me through my panic. I learned to swim in about thirty seconds. How come it takes two weeks for a professional to teach a kid how to swim? All I needed was someone's mom.

I raced home to tell my parents that I had learned to swim, and they were grand with that. If a neighbor threw a kid who couldn't swim into a pool in 2020 it would be on cable news an hour later and they would be charged with assault.

Author's Warning: This method hasn't been officially approved by the Academy of Swimming Teachers. Please do not teach your neighbor's kids this way. The author is not responsible for the actions of anyone who replicates anything I have written about in this book.

I wonder if sometimes all the specialized training just gets in our way and all we needed was the common sense of a mom or a dad. In my thirty years of educational hiring, the best person for most jobs was usually the best human being, not the person with the most technical expertise. We could provide training for technical expertise, but the training for how to be a good human being took a lot longer.

PS: Please hold the angry emails about wanting a trained airline pilot or surgeon and not just someone's mom flying the plane or performing surgery. Obviously, there are *many* specific times when I only want a highly trained person and don't care if they are a complete jerk. I'm just saying... sometimes the neighbor's mom or dad can give our kids fairly good advice or teach our kids to hit a baseball. We don't always need a professional.

Save your breath
Kevin and I had spent the day with a team from another school district talking about restorative justice. I was the lead person and invited Kevin for support. I spent the day passionately explaining how important RJ was. It wasn't just about teaching kids the communication and social skills to get along in this world, it was also about ending exclusionary discipline policies that took a toll on poor and minority students. I felt I was persuasive and visionary. Kevin, a middle school counselor, just calmly answered questions and explained how it might work if you ever decided to give it a shot. He didn't really have much invested in whether another school district adopted the program or not.

The next day, we had an email from the school principal thanking us for such a great day and saying the staff wanted to give it a try. They especially liked Kevin's approach.

What the heck? I was the student services director who had

successfully implemented restorative justice in a challenging school for over ten years. I only invited Kevin along for someone to talk with on the long drive. We always had awesome conversations. To add insult to injury, the principal was my brother in law! I was totally annoyed. As I thought about it for a while though, I realized for about the 5000th time in my life that people are much more likely to listen to someone who isn't as invested or persuasive. A take it or leave it approach usually works best.

It didn't take long at all after beginning my first principalship to realize that nobody was all that interested in my advice. I had to relearn the lesson frequently though. I'm reasonably adept at staying in my own lane, and don't tend to give much advice, much to Laketa's chagrin when we were raising teens. However, when the plaque stating, "Steve Morse, Principal" was stuck on my desk, I felt an internal pressure building inside of me to weigh in more frequently. After all, I was the big boss now. The students depended on me bossing around the teachers to have any type of future at all! I had been primed with the message that the principal made the biggest difference in a school throughout my program for principal certification. The professors made it sound like we needed to be giving constant feedback to keep the school from falling apart. I was trying on a new hat by trying to give more advice.

I was 34 years old at the time with ten years of teaching experience and five years of parenting under my belt. You can imagine how excited the 20-30+ year veteran teachers and the parents in town would be to hear all the current information that I picked up while obtaining my degree. I'll pause here for a minute while I let you guess how enthused they were … (tick, tick, tick…) My initial year reminded me of a sign I saw perusing a shop at the beach, "How come people who think they know everything never know when to shut up."

Every single year for the next 29 years as an administrator, I learned to give less and less advice. My learning curve went like this. Stage 1: I need to attempt to give every staff member a piece of wisdom at least a couple of times a month. I'm the principal! Stage 2: I need to determine how to prioritize my counsel and only give each staff member the most relevant guidance several times a year. Stage 3: Unless it is at least a semi-serious teaching, safety, or student rights issue, I am only going to give advice when asked specifically for it by the teacher. Stage 4: Rarely give advice. When asked for advice directly, send it back to the asker with questions like. "What have you tried in the past? What are you thinking about trying? What seems to motivate the kid? etc."

99 out of 100 times the person came up with a solution that was either similar to what I was thinking or better. People have incrementally more willingness to try a new strategy when it is their own idea. If it works, they are proud they figured it out themselves and gain confidence. If it doesn't work, they/we can try plan B. There was certainly no money back guarantee that my idea would have worked any better. Kids are complex and no two kids respond the same way.

People almost always know what they are going to do before they ask for advice. They want the hearer to confirm what they are already thinking and rarely follow the counsel given, unless it is similar to what they wanted to hear in the first place. Arguments and Facebook posts usually just make people dig in harder to what they already believed and most of us hear what we want to hear. The principalship required me to hear and empathize with divergent viewpoints multiple times a day. Everyone approaches a problem differently and their way might work better for them than my way.

Thomas Plante, Ph.D., in ABPP at Santa Clara University, in an article in *Psychology Today* in July of 2014, shares why giving advice rarely works. He makes the obvious point that modeling is almost the only way to influence people. We rehearse convincing arguments in our heads to sway people politically religiously, etc. and it rarely, if ever, works. He also admits the paradox and blatant hypocrisy of giving people the advice to stop giving advice.

It was actually kind of a relief for me to not feel constant pressure to give everyone a bunch of advice that they would never use anyway. I've always found that I have enough problems of my own without telling everyone else what to do. It was much more natural for me to get to the point of giving less advice.

Giving myself permission to relax with my spouse, kids, and the people I worked with really took the lid off the kettle at work and at home during teen years. My family and the teachers I supervised seemed to survive ok without my constant two cents' worth and wouldn't have taken my counsel at the given time anyway. Modeling and loving unconditionally are by far the best approaches, followed by empathizing, listening, working together collaboratively, and trying to learn and grow myself.

I can't control the speed at which others grow, but eventually most people will be fine and figure stuff out eventually. My teenage kids weren't interested in a lot of advice in high school but seem to have figured most of it out by age 25. I'm hoping my love, support, and modeling helped a little bit but doubt my advice was a big game changer on any given day.

I never met a man I didn't like ... Will Rogers, 1926
(or a woman ... revised by Steve Morse, 2020)

The will Rogers' quote for this section was definitely true for me, once adapted for women. I am friends with everybody.

A co-worker asked me who my best friend was a couple of years ago. I gave it some thought before realizing that I don't think of friendship the way I used to. As a kid, I knew who my best pals were at any given time and could name the fifteen others in my posse in rank order.

When I was in high school and college, I developed friendships that were deep and spent a lot of time with friends. When Laketa and I first married we moved to a small town in Eastern Washington, and I missed my old friends severely. We were lonely there, especially at first. I lamented the fact that I wasn't developing the type of close friendships like I had in college.

Laketa reminded me that the nature of friendships probably would be different post-college. After a year, we developed several close friends there, but college is still a unique time of life. You live together 24/7 right when you are in an intense period of human growth. While I don't have the same intensity of soul mates as I had in college, I still have many meaningful friendships that are much deeper in different ways.

I have heard the job of principal described as similar to a pastor in a small town. I found that to be true and quickly developed strong and meaningful relationships with the parents and teachers in all four schools where I served as principal. There is a close bond that develops when you are engaged collaboratively in meaningful work. Even when I did the eight-month principal substitute job, I grew close to the staff and families after only a couple of months.

I had a college best friend that I only attended school with for one year. He was from Florida and now lives in Chicago have seen him exactly twice in the last 45 years, and both times we picked up right where we left off. It felt as if I had seen him the day before and as if he was still my best friend.

Almost every secretary I worked with became close friends

with Laketa and me, also. They were all good human beings, and when someone has your back like that, it's hard not to appreciate them and feel like they are your friend. With all the "uniquely Steve" decisions I made at work; my secretaries constantly saved my bacon.

We made friends in Lynden, moved away, and didn't see them much again for over twenty years. We reconnected recently and are close friends with them again. I have companions that I play pickleball and tennis with whom I have never once seen off the court but consider good friends. I even met a neighbor thirty years younger than me who I instantly hit it off with. He asked Laketa and me to be the two witnesses at his wedding. He moved, and we may never see him again, but I still feel a connection to him and call him a good friend.

A couple of my absolute best friends in the world live four hours away and even though I rarely see them, I feel a close connection. My definition of friendship has evolved. I don't have to be with a person ten to twelve hours a week to consider them a close friend and I know any of the people listed in this paragraph would be at my home in a New York minute if I needed them, and I would do the same.

I played tennis with this one guy several times a week every summer for about ten years. We never talked off the tennis courts and we never called or emailed to check on each other in the winter. After an eight-month hiatus every year, I called him, and the conversation went something like this.
Me: This is Steve. Tennis?
Him: Yes.
Me: Fifteen minutes?
Him: Yes
Click.

Laketa would look at me and nod her head and tell me how weird guy friendships were. "You don't even say hello or ask how the other person is doing? You don't ask about his family? Do you know if he even has a family? Does he even know you have a family?"

After we had been playing about six years, he had concerns about how the school was handling his child. We leaned against the fence after our matches and talked a lot during this time. We just never needed to talk until then! As an educator, I was able to offer both suggestions on what to tell the school and encouragement that this too would pass. It did. His kid is doing great now.

Long story long, my view of relationships and best friends has significantly evolved. If someone asked me now who my best friend is, I would answer that I feel blessed to have literally hundreds of close friends. They all play different roles and some I rarely see, but care about them just as much.

When Jedediah Jenkins was asked the same question, she answered by saying, "I don't know. I don't use language like that anymore. It doesn't fit. I have friends who hold the keys to different doors of my personality. Some open my heart. Some my laughter. Some my mischief. Some my sin. Some my civic urgency. Some my history. Some my rawest confusion and vulnerability. Some, who may be as close as my skin, may not have what I need today. It's ok if our spouses or partners don't have every key. How could they? It isn't a failure if they don't open every key of who you are. The million-room-mansion of identity cannot overlap perfectly with anyone. But I will say, my closest friends have a key ring on their hip with lots of keys jingling."

Laketa was right when she suggested that I stop mourning the loss of college-type relationships and work on what I have now. I needed to open my eyes and look at what is right in front of my face. My friendships are significantly deeper and closer now.

Enough already

I love people who:

- Blurt out something way too personal in group settings.
- Walk around with a ketchup stain on their shirt.
- Start chuckling to themselves and no one else knows why.
- Laugh loudly at their own jokes.
- Tell the same stories over and over.
- Make friends in the grocery line.

I suppose the reason I like people like that is because I'm like that. Whenever a new teacher laughed at one of my jokes, one of the veteran (let's be honest; old, but they always made me say experienced or veteran) teachers admonished them not to do that, as it usually led to repetition of the same dumb joke.

One day at work while I was rambling away at my desk, one of the secretaries in our shared office space announced, "You know, Steve, you don't have to say every little thing that pops into your head."

After my initial irritation, I realized she might have a point. Perhaps I hadn't given this as much thought as the situation warranted. People enjoyed working with me because I was funny. Kids, families, and staff members loved my stories, but ... I did seem to have to say every little thing that popped into my head. Maybe it was enough already. If she reads this book, she'll probably email me and say, "You know, Steve, you didn't have to write every little thing that popped into your head."

I decided to try her strategy for a while. I instituted the STFU initiative for district level meetings. I attempted to STFU (shut the f*** up) for the next couple of months in our district-wide meetings. Not all day, mind you. That would be way too hard for a talker like me. Just in the whole group affairs. Whenever I started to talk, I started scribbling STFU (the acronym, not all the words!) over and over on my note pad. It looked as if I was taking copious notes and paying close attention. The initiative was a roaring success.

I am attempting to initiate the STFU strategy in my personal life, also. Polling in my household shows 100 percent approval for this initiative. I'm still working on it, and I think I'm improving, but household polling might not support my beliefs.

You have two ears and one mouth

I've always been an enthusiastic conversationalist. Quietly listening is a struggle for me. However, near the end of my career I developed a reputation for being a great listener, in certain situations. I beamed when my boss told the retirement dinner attendees that listening was my superpower. It always makes me feel proud to improve at something that is a challenge.

Besides wanting to make everyone laugh, part of my listening problem was that it's always been important to me to connect closely with others. My brain immediately starts to scan for areas of connection or common ground. I learned to recognize when people needed to be heard and understood, not connect.

I learned this lesson the hard way. Upset parents don't respond well if they think the principal isn't listening. I had to (and still have to) focus my brain to listen prior to meeting to succeed. It doesn't come naturally for me. Parents and teachers helped me learn to see things from others perspective and realize that my perspective might only be "my" perspective. I often set a goal to not speak at all until people could take that deep breath of knowing they were completely heard.

Thoroughly listening the first time, no matter how long it took, saved time in the long run. This approach was especially helpful when I was meeting with a minority parent about a disciplinary situation concerning their child. Data indicates that the school system generally over-disciplines minority kids. That was probably even more true when the child's parents were in school. They were coming to me with a history of feeling like the school system was biased and wanted me to listen carefully, not dismiss their concerns or try to resonate with how they felt.

I recognized that when they told me that I didn't understand, they were right. I knew I didn't understand. Our system has blind spots, and I do individually, also. After they felt heard, my next step was to ask them for suggestions for solving the issue. I tried to get them to realize that the school and I, the principal, wanted the same outcome as they wanted. We all wanted a happy successful child. Let's work together to figure this out.

I always avoided defending the situation or arguing. A defensive approach of, "I'm not racist. The school did nothing wrong.", would never get me anywhere. I listened fully, avoided assigning blame, and took an approach of "let's fix this together", without getting into fault or who was and wasn't racist at our school. I acknowledged the implicit bias and systemic issues without accusing a specific staff member of being racist by taking the approach that we all had a ton to learn, including me.

Now and again, I would tell one of my stories after they had put everything on the table, and I was certain they were completely heard. I found this built rapport and most families and kids with school troubles appreciated those stories. Word spread that I listen, and I "got" kids who had trouble in school, because I had some of the same issues when I was a kid.

At one time, several African American families were asking to transfer to Roosevelt. When I asked them why, they said word on the street was that Roosevelt School treated minority kids fairly and the principal "got it". As a 45-year-old white male who knew I didn't really "get it", this was humbling. Ironically, by admitting I didn't get it, I "got it". Often educators are afraid to admit we don't get it, because we are afraid people will think we might be racist. Educators may also be afraid to admit there is implicit bias in "their" school or their classroom, even though we acknowledge it is in every other school, due to fear it will be used against them.

The first time I met with an upset minority parent as a principal in 1989 in Westport, I argued with the parent and denied that the school was racist or had done anything wrong. I knew I was right, and this kid was a really challenging student. I needed Mom to listen to me.

My superintendent attended the meeting with me and afterwards told me that I just should have just listened, even if the school wasn't technically "at fault" in this situation. It was my first month working with him and we hadn't developed a close relationship yet, so his advice irritated the heck out of me. Ironically, I ended up giving this exact recommendation to Roosevelt teachers prior to every single parent meeting for thirteen years. If I ever see him again, I'll apologize for getting irritated with him and say, "Thanks.". That meeting did not go well, and his mom stormed out angrily, slamming the door as she left. We never were able to work as a team to help her child and she despised me from that day forward. She also let everyone know what a jerk I was.

Another, "listening" strategy I used was that I intentionally "lost" 100 percent of first-time suspension appeals. When a parent appealed a suspension, I listened without speaking or defending the suspension until they ran out of steam. I then announced, "Congratulations. You won the appeal. I will reduce the suspension to time served. Bring your child back to school thirty minutes early tomorrow and we can set up a plan to help your child be successful."

At the planning meeting, I informed the parent that if the child committed that particular offense again, they wouldn't win the appeal the second time. We didn't suspend kids very often and to get suspended took a serious enough offense that we couldn't allow that behavior to continue unabated. They invariably gave their blessing to that, and I don't recall anyone appealing for the same offense again. Here is my favorite story about how listening empathetically to a parent changed the situation completely.

Paul came to Roosevelt at age seven on a bus from a metropolitan city in the south. He had been living with his mom there and hadn't met his father, who lived in Bellingham. Mom left him with a younger sibling and a loaded pistol when she went to work every night, with instructions to use it if anyone attempted to get in the house. Dad had been a boy soldier in Africa, so he was dealing with a great deal of childhood trauma and was homeless at the time.

Paul had significant behavioral issues and had been told to never trust white people. Our staff had 38 white people and two Latino people, so Paul was up a creek with no paddle on that issue. He was big, strong, and coordinated for a seven-year old, but either hadn't been to school yet or hadn't been emotionally available to learn much when attending. We weren't sure and never were able to get school records. When we assessed hum, he still wasn't even at a first month kindergarten level. Our policy was to put kids in the correct grade level by age 99.9 percent of the time, regardless of academic skill. We assumed it was our job to catch them up, and the research on holding kids back a grade suggests that it harms students more often than it helps.

However, in this case, Ms. Del Wraa volunteered to have him in her first-grade class with the plan of keeping him for two years, as she was taking her entire class to second grade with her the next year. She quickly grew to love Paul and he walked to her house for dinner a couple of times a week over the next six years. He ended up moving to Nebraska, but still visits her every time he comes back to town. Ms. Del Wraa was one of many teachers at Roosevelt who always volunteered to take the most challenging students. Roosevelt really was (and still is) a special place.

Paul was one angry kid. One of the behavioral specialists from the district, who came to consult with us, claimed he could throw a chair further than anyone she had seen in all her years in that position. He could literally throw a chair all the way across the commons area and hit the wall in the air! I wanted to try after school one day to see if I could do it but was wise enough (barely) to follow the advice of several teachers asking me not to do that. I still think I could have hit the top of the wall though.

Paul struggled during his time at Roosevelt, but Ms. Del Wraa and his teachers over the next four years loved and supported him. He took part in all our field trips and extracurricular activities. He was quite charismatic, and the other students liked him. That was a bonus, as kids with behavioral issues only behave even more poorly when everyone else hates them. He loved helping younger kids and that was good therapy for him. We let him volunteer, while being closely monitored, in kindergarten. He looked like a celebrity walking to the bus every day with all the kindergarten kids running up to high-five him while yelling, "Paul, Paul."

Ms. Del Wraa became like a mom to Paul. She was firm and expected him to do well but had a mother's touch. She gave him lots of hugs and told him he was too good of a person to do the things he did when he screwed up. One time he punched her as hard as he could in the stomach. She got down eye to eye with him and told him in no uncertain terms that he was never ever to hit a woman again, as long as he walked this earth. He teared up and he never touched a teacher again. She didn't tell me for a few weeks when this happened, because she was worried that I might suspend him. She wanted to work it out herself and let Paul know she would love him unconditionally, no matter what he did.

After a few months, his dad called to meet with me because he thought Ms. Del Wraa was punishing Paul unfairly because Paul was black. I had a hard time not immediately arguing that point, as Ms. Del Wraa was loving this kid to the moon, he went to her house for dinner, and she hadn't even sent him to the office when he punched her in the stomach. That didn't appear overly harsh to me. Paul was devoted to her and I doubt you could find a jury that would say she was punishing him unfairly. However, I stuck with my approach.

Ms. Del Wraa wasn't too thrilled about being accused of being unfair due to race when she was going about forty miles above and beyond with Paul on a daily basis. She almost hit the ceiling stating "Are you kidding! This is what I get after all I've done for him!"

Luckily, this was about my fifteenth year of being a principal, and I had learned to listen to parents nondefensively. I let her know my strategy, which she wasn't too excited about.

"So, let me get this straight. You're not going to even defend me? You're not going to point out all the extra things I've done or say that you don't think I'm a racist? You don't want me to defend myself? You want to just sit and listen?"

Well, when you put it that way… Anyways, she agreed to the strategy, and I told her I would sit next to her and kick her under the table when it was most likely she would want to correct dad. I couldn't have kicked just any teacher, but Ms. D and I had a good working relationship.

Dad couldn't meet until late on a Friday, as he didn't have the type of job that he could trade time for. So, to add insult to injury, Ms. D had to stay a couple of hours late on a Friday evening for the opportunity to be accused of being a racist. Dad had a rich British African accent and spent about 45 minutes telling his story, beginning with his childhood. It was fascinating to listen to and incredibly heartbreaking. I felt as if we were sitting around a campfire while he recounted what he and Paul had been through and shared his hopes for a better life for his son. Dad could deliver an awesome Ted talk if he could cut his speech to twenty minutes.

I needed to kick Ms. D about six or seven times when he recounted incidents at school that were almost 180 degrees the opposite of what we observed, but she managed to just sit and listen. Several times he would stop and start a paragraph over. We wondered later if he had spent the time to memorize a 45-minute monologue. Growing up as a boy soldier, his literacy skills were probably low, and his culture has a strong oral tradition. This was later confirmed by our secretary when she found out he had been driving without a license because he couldn't take the test. She also found out he let Paul drive sometimes, even though Paul was ten at that time.

Paul's dad wasn't in a hurry at all, whereas most people in our culture would try to get right to the point. His story is still my favorite oral story I have ever heard.

When he finished his narrative, there was complete silence for about sixty seconds, as we were the only three people still in the building. We were so choked up that I wasn't sure either of us would be able to speak. Finally, I squeaked out, "Thank you so much for taking the time to talk with us. I'm so sorry for what you and Paul have been through. Barb and I will commit to do anything we can to help. What would you like us to do?" I didn't defend our actions, I didn't correct the misconceptions in his story, I didn't tell him about the diversity training we had, I didn't tell him Barb and I weren't racist. Nada. Silence.

He sat quietly for another full minute or two, and then with tears running down both his cheeks, he said, "I don't know. Please help me." He then put one hand over each of our hands and held it there on the table.

At this point we worked together to develop a plan and continued to work closely with Paul for the next four years. We continued a warm and collegial relationship with dad all the way through, and I looked forward to his two handed, thirty second handshakes and sincere smiles when he came to evening events with Paul. In my forty-year career, the work with Paul and his dad was my most rewarding relationship.

We had several other similar situations with African American families. Each of them was unique, but through listening with zero defensiveness for as long as it took and by collaborating closely with the parent's, we made progress and kept the kids in school. All six or seven of the kids with similar situations graduated high school and most came back to visit the teachers and me a few times during their high school years.

I'm a gregarious person and I still have to check myself and be aware not to monopolize conversations. When I manage to just be quiet and listen, situations turn out all right though. Watching the Black Lives Matter protests made me realize once again the importance of seeing and hearing people. Protestors wanted to be seen and heard badly enough to risk catching Covid-19. I fear our society will never get past our racial issues a without an intensive round of non-defensive listening.

In the meantime, I'm going to keep practicing being a better listener and hope I can get to a place in my personal life similar to where I got at work. Home is always harder than just having to gear up for a thirty-minute session now and again at work.

Don't be Al Capone
A work colleague gave me this career admonition many times. Whenever I decided to skip some bureaucratic BS, Keith would quietly say "Don't be Al Capone." He told me the story of how Al Capone was never convicted for murder or his other heinous crimes but ended up getting put away for tax evasion. Al forgot

to dot his i's and cross his t's.

My strengths were my relationships with people, especially kids, but I was always tempted to skip what seemed like mindless BS paperwork. Keith reminded me to complete the tasks that might get me fired for not doing, like federal paperwork or annual teacher evaluations. Don't go to prison for tax evasion!

I completed these tasks quickly though, as I didn't write a doctoral thesis for every assignment. I wasn't concerned if a bureaucrat in Washington, DC, gave me an A+ or C-. I decided to grade myself pass/fail on this type of work. Also, I wasn't completely sure any of these were ever read. I certainly never got any indication that they were. No one at the central office or in DC ever called to say, "We got your paperwork and it was really good."

When I moved to the central office there were even more of these types of annoying tasks. Whenever I was mumbling and grumbling and trying to decide whether to do something or skip it, Keith quietly stated, "Don't be Al Capone", without even looking up from his laptop. That was all I needed to hear. I banged something out in ten minutes, and I didn't get fired in three decades of school administration! I'm retired now but will still encounter a few Al Capone moments. I wonder if I could pay Keith to set up a desk in the corner of our condo and work quietly there without bothering me until I need him.

I'm not really a morning person

I was never much of a morning person. I could sleep until noon in high school and college with no problem at all. When Laketa and I got married, she was surprised how grumpy I was every morning. I seemed so nice before we got married. As fate would have it, she loved the mornings and started chirping away happily about thirty seconds after she woke up. I grunted like a cave man in return until about noon.

In the evening though, I was rearing to go! I wanted to hit the town and couldn't stop talking about everything that had happened at work that day. Unfortunately, she liked to settle in, read, and just have quiet time at night. That caused a certain amount of low-level friction for us for years. Now we are both exhausted morning and at night, so it works perfectly.

When I taught third grade in Lynden school started at 7:45, and the kids poured noisily into the room at 7:30. I could barely function, but they knew not to mess with me for the first hour or so.

When I became a principal, I always worked more than forty hours a week, so I gave myself permission to stumble in groggily a few minutes late most mornings. I usually got out of bed about half an hour before my official start time. That kind of cracked everyone up, but I was doing a good job and working plenty of hours, so nobody busted my chops too much. I did get a lot of teasing about my unkempt hair and occasional inside-out shirt though.

In my mid-40s, having two teens and working my butt off as a principal, I started to be much less of a night owl. I could no longer honestly describe myself as a night person. I still wasn't a morning person, so I started describing myself as an afternoon person.

The last five years of work in the central office, I started getting much less interested in attending some lame meeting after about 2:30. I complained to my secretary, Nancy, about scheduling a difficult parent for 4:00. "I don't really have the energy for an emotional conference at 4:00.", I stated.

"Interesting. Last week you told me you aren't a morning person and didn't want to have to face an angry parent early in the morning. Shall I tell everyone I can schedule you between 10:00-2:00, as long as it doesn't bump into your one-hour lunch?", she asked.

I thought that was the perfect plan! Unfortunately, Nancy didn't agree. Good thing I was retiring soon.

At least Laketa and I are finally in perfect sync. If you would like to get together with us, call between about 10:00 and 2:00, but not during lunch or nap time!

Don't trip going down the stairs

My final year of work I decided to leave about two o'clock on a sunny Friday afternoon. I was feeling giddy, like Ferris Bueller skipping school. I scooped up my laptop and headed for the back stairway. I was so excited that I wasn't paying attention going down the stairs. I lost my footing about six or seven steps from the landing. Even though I had zero think time, I reflexively knew the best strategy would be to leap for the landing, rather than tumbling down the final six or seven stairs. I soared through the air like Michael Jordan and tossed my laptop over the back of my head. When I hit, I rolled through the crash. The laptop barely missed my head as it crashed behind me. The noise from the fall was unbelievably loud. How could one guy and a laptop make that much noise!

Pretty much every person in the entire building came running to see if I was okay, including the superintendent and my direct supervisor. So much for sneaking out. People tried to convince me to go to the ER, as the fall was so loud. The superintendent sat with me for about ten minutes while I caught my breath. It was a little challenging to make small talk after being caught in the act of sneaking down the back staircase. I'm the worst sneaker-outer in the world, and never would have made it as a spy. That never even showed up on my list when I was a little kid.

The superintendent directed the wellness director to immediately put signage up on every staircase exhorting us to be cautious. Of course, everyone knew it was me and some smart aleck put a photo of my head on each of the posters. I got mocked from that day on until I retired. I couldn't leave the office without someone telling me to be careful going down the stairs while everyone else snickered. One of the women was even upset that I didn't break something, as she had broken her ankle on a much lower stair fall earlier that year. Thanks for all the support, workmates.

Last week, I was hiking in the Washington drizzle when I came to a long staircase down a cliff to the beach. It looked slippery, but had a sturdy handrail along the side, so I started down the stairs. It was a terrifying trek, and I was relieved to make it to the beach without breaking my neck, as my cell phone didn't work at this location and I was hiking alone. (I know, I know. Don't send a bunch of emails telling me to never hike alone.)

When it came time to leave, the stairs looked daunting. It was steep and I needed to rest a time or two on the way up. I made it to the top and began the flat part of the hike back to the car. As I was walking, I started reflecting on how that staircase was such a great metaphor for my life.

I thought back to the struggles in my life and how I worried about getting through them. I got tired and needed to stop and rest on the way up. Unfortunately, though, most of the danger in my life came on my way down the stairs. My biggest falls and failures usually happened when I was coasting or on a more comfortable path, not when I was struggling to get to the next plateau. This happened at work frequently. When times were tough, I struggled to reach the next level, or at least survive, but I got more complacent when things were going well.

I was concerned that I might get complacent and bored in retirement. I would find out soon enough.

RETIRED LIFE
... 2020-??

We were eating dinner when Lianne told Cruz he would be going to preschool next year. Cruz replied, "I'll miss you, Mama, but Nana and Papa will be going to school with me." He's told me that again a few times since then. I'm sure I will volunteer now and again, but after sixty years in school, am I really going to spend the next thirteen years in school with Cruz. Aye caramba.

So, what now? I have been in school since 1960. My career brought a lot of joy into my life and my work in the schools reached my soul in ways that few other places could. Will I be able to stay busy and keep learning? Will I feel like the NBA and MLB players playing in an empty stadium? Time to find out.

FOMO No Mo'
An acquaintance posted this on social media a few weeks ago. "Live the life you have, not the life you wish you had." That hit me like a punch to the solar plexus. I have been repeating it as a mantra whenever I wish I were somewhere else or doing something else for a few months now, which is much too often for a retired guy. You would think I might mature over time.

I was introduced to the term FOMO (fear of missing out) for the first-time last year. I realized that I have suffered from this disease my entire life. No matter what I am doing, I wonder what other people are doing and if that would be more fun. FOMO is my personal nemesis to being mindful and living my life one moment at a time.

A couple of months ago I was involved in an awesome game of pickleball. In my mind, I was in the world championships. I couldn't stop smiling and thinking that this retirement gig was pretty darn nice. I was playing exceptionally well, at least for me.
Nonetheless, I found myself looking over to the court next to us between points. It looked as if they were having an even better game than we were. I started wishing I were on that court. Good grief! I'm over sixty years old and still haven't learned to savor where I am and enjoy what I am doing, even when what I am doing is awesome. I seem to be always looking for something better. The "angle man" story came back to me from my college days.

Social media is a strong contributor to this disease. Seeing my friends and relatives on vacation and hearing about how their kid just scored the winning touchdown doesn't help me live in the moment. Not many people put a post on when they are having a lousy day, or their kid just got suspended from school. In our advanced society, I now have the ability right at my fingertips to be jealous of others and unhappy from the comfort of my own living room. Isn't technology grand!

I remember when we moved to Lynden, Washington, in 1984. It was a religiously conservative town, and we were warned not to do any loud chores outside on a Sunday, because we would offend the neighbors. We also needed to get groceries on Saturday, as everything was closed Sunday. I thought this was the stupidest thing I had ever heard. Good grief, it's 1984, not 1650. I hid behind my fence to paint the back side on Sunday and painted the front of it on Monday. Another opportunity to practice the skill of looking like I was following the rules when I wasn't.

After a few months though, I completely changed my tune. I

started to absolutely love Sundays. I could ride my bike right down main street with no hands. I had time for long strolls, reading, napping, breathing, seeing neighbors. Not being able to do yard work or go shopping was paradise. At the time, I was coaching, getting a master's degree one evening a week, and working another two evenings a week cleaning a bank and mini mall to pay for the degree. Not being "allowed" to do anything on Sunday was the best thing to happen to me in a long time. It was the best excuse to give Laketa that I had found to that point, too.

Prior to moving, I was coaching and working about seventy hours a week. We drove 25 miles after a few hours in church on Sunday afternoons to do our weekly shopping. I started to hate every Sunday. Upon reflection, I realized that I hadn't liked Sundays my whole life except for during football season. Since moving to Lynden, I was looking forward to Sundays for the first time in my life. It was an actual day of rest. I haven't been dogmatic about it but have rarely done anything remotely resembling work on Sunday since 1984. Although, some might argue that I rarely ever did anything remotely resembling work on the other six days, too. My last secretary missed my retirement celebration because she thought I had retired a year or two earlier and was just hanging around the office.

When the governor mandated social isolation, it was easier to beat FOMO at first, as I had no choice. I kind of liked not having to worry about what anyone else was doing. It gave me lots of opportunities to practice letting go and just living the life in front of me. It didn't take long for FOMO to return though.

I heard on the radio last spring that ninety percent of people think their life will be better in ten years. This is called the fallacy of arrival. Ten years later, they still think their life will be better in ten more years. Most of us live our whole lives like this and never quite arrive.

PH. D Nate Holden warns us, "Beware of destination addiction, a preoccupation with the idea that happiness is in the next place, the next job and with the next partner. Until you give up on the idea that happiness is somewhere else, it will never be where you are."

Winnie the pooh: What day is it?
Piglet. It's today:
Pooh: My favorite day
A.A. Milne

Look, Papa, look.

I love spending time with Cruz, my two-year old grandkid. He shows me the world through new eyes. Everything is exciting. Every activity we do is akin to my excitement level at an all you can eat buffet. Looking at the moon, seeing a bird, watching a motorcycle or the garbage truck drive by are all equally thrilling. I'm discovering how to see everything around me with new eyes again. This has been especially helpful during the pandemic. I never knew how much there was to see within a couple of blocks of our condo.

I've noticed how urgent it is for Cruz to be seen. No time to wait. I hear the phrase "Look, Papa, look.", about every two minutes the whole time we are together. If I don't look quickly enough, he adds, "I'm right here, Papa. I'm right here." He reminds me how much we want to be seen.

I want others to understand and see me. I've just learned not to say it every minute or two. Parents often asked me why I thought the kids liked me so much. I usually said, "If you want to be a kid magnet, see them, hear them, play with them.". Kids know when you see them. Seeing and listening builds instant rapport.

My transition to a central office job about killed me. I didn't get to hear, "I love you, Mr. Morse.", ten to twenty times a day. I made the mistake of telling a few people at work I missed that, and some wise guy told me that he loved me every time he saw me for a few months. Thanks a lot, Brian.

I read an article a few years back about a study where researchers went to playgrounds to observe the behavior of parents. Many parents were looking at their cell phones most of the time. The kids kept yelling, "Look at me.", as they slid down slides and scrambled over the monkey bars. The parents would glance up for a second and smile and then return to their phones.

As a kid, I was a total pain in the ass from the moment I opened my eyes in the morning until I fell asleep that night. I seemed to have this intense need for someone to see me, hear me, and understand me. I guess I haven't changed too much, because now I'm writing a book! Hear me! Listen! Even when the principal let me lead that assembly in the fourth grade, I only felt satisfied with my need for attention for about five minutes before I started pestering her to schedule another one.

I wanted to be seen so badly that I was willing to take any punishment, including significant physical pain. Corporal punishment at school has been illegal in Washington since 1989 but was alive and well when I attended. Even though those swats hurt like mad, I was willing to take a swat to gain the adoration and attention of my peers on a regular basis. People saw me and noticed me that day. Lots of head nods and high-fives all day long.

In the seventh grade, I had a PE teacher who had biceps about as big as my thighs when I became an adult. I got quite a few swats from him. He made me stand in front of a mirror so I could see my pain visually. The third time I was waiting to get hammered by him, I was a little more nervous than usual. He told me that he was really going to nail me for this third one, as I hadn't learned anything yet. I was sweating bullets.

My classmates convinced me to keep my PE shorts on under my jeans for that swat. As I bent over, Mr. T said, "Oh, it looks like you forgot to remove your shorts. That's too bad. I guess I'll have to give a little harder swing." Aye caramba. My stomach flipped just now remembering the pain. It hurt so much that I waited a couple of more weeks to regain my courage to get another swat.

Two friends and I had a contest to see who could get the most swats in seventh grade. We each put $20 in a pot for the winner to take at the end of the year. I worked hard on my paper route to save the money. Those knuckleheads probably snuck the money out of their mom's purse to get their stake. Minimum wage was $1.25 in the mid-60's, so that would be the equivalent of over $600 now. Not too shabby for a seventh-grade kid.

This was also the same year Grease Gun and I were having a contest to see who could eat all 32 sundaes on the menu at the corner Big Scoop first, so I desperately needed the money. It was only October, so I only had seventeen swats at the time of this debacle. Dave had sixteen and Jack had nineteen. The principal called us into his office, "I hear you boneheads are having a contest to see who can get the most swats."

We looked at each other nervously, but no one squealed. A minute or two of deafening silence passed before he said, "I have instructed the teachers not to give you any more swats." Jack leaped from his chair and started dancing around the room yelling, "I won! I won! Bring the money tomorrow."

Dave and I fell to our knees begging Mr. H to give us one more week. "Please, Mr. H, I'm out of verbal warnings in several of my classes. I know I could get several more swats by the end of the week. It's not fair to just end the contest with no warning. How about just two more weeks."

In my mind, this would be the equivalent of a referee saying the game is over when there were two minutes left on the clock and my team was at the one-yard line. For all my other problems, I had a keen sense of justice and this was morally wrong. The principal would not reverse his decision though and that was my last swat until the next fall. Jack pocketed the money, I lost another $20 on the sundae contest, and my popularity took a nose-dive. It was a horrible morning overall. I still get upset when I remember this story. When I was a principal, I never made a major change in policy without a warning to the kids. It wasn't fair and I would have given the kids at least one more week.

A few seconds of excruciating pain was a great trade for popularity. I've analyzed my dysfunctional childhood in other parts of this book, but the point here is ... Everyone, regardless of age, wants to be seen and will do almost anything to be seen and understood. Most people will either find a way to be seen or give up at some point in their lives.

Not many adults yell "Look at me!" all the time, but they still want to be seen. Charles Finn makes the case that even hearing is primarily a visual experience in his book," Please Hear What I'm Not Saying". We listen with more than our ears, and people realize they are being heard by the way we use our eyes and body language. The actual words are a small part of our communications.

The Mobile Response Team for our district is deployed to a school when a student commits suicide or dies in an accident. New members worried about what to say. Jeff, the team leader, responded with, "You don't have to say anything, just listen and be with them." Jeff followed this with a story about being at a funeral when he was in elementary school. His father told him to go sit with a boy who had lost his dad. Jeff told his father, "I don't know what to say."

His father replied, "Don't say anything. Just go and sit by him. Be with him." The retelling of that story to new team members affected me every year.

I know another person who said that he crawled under his bed whenever he was upset as a child. His mom would crawl in next to him and just lay there with him without saying a word. She was just with him.

In her book, "The World that We Knew", Alice Hoffman writes about a painter asking his friend what color the sky was. When she told him it was black, the painter said, "You need to look more closely." We all need to look more closely at those around us.

Even though it is late in my life, I'm thankful that Cruz is helping me to learn to "Look, Papa, look."

Damn it

I grew up in a family where I never heard my parents swear, take a sip of alcohol, or smoke a cigarette. I also never heard the "L word", but I already told that story. I almost never swore until I was about fifty years old. At that point, I figured I was relatively safe from falling into a life of disrepute over a cuss word or two. Furthermore, there were many situations where swearing seemed like the most appropriate way to express the emotion I was feeling. Initially, this really cracked people up, as most had never heard me cuss before that. True to form, the laughter encouraged me to double down on my swearing.

After a few months of pouring it on big time, Laketa told me that it wasn't all that commendable for a 50+ year old elementary school principal to swear like a logger. I apologize to any loggers reading this book, especially Killer, but you have to admit that you earned that reputation! Laketa grew especially weary of the "f" word, even though I used that epitaph more sparingly.

After initial irritation with her suggestion, I decided she was probably right. I determined I would scale back a bit, reserving the best words for just the right situations. That would give me more power per cuss word. In my humble opinion, I think I've nailed it now and have discovered the perfect level of swearing. Now that I have a grandson though, I need to be a little more cautious about timing.
.

Most kids and standup comedians use the f word" much too often, in my opinion. It's a bit painful to listen to and not a dialogue to which I aspire. It's way more impactful when used sparingly and in the most appropriate situations where it just fits like a glove.

Our superintendent officiated a memorial service for a beloved and respected principal who passed tragically before her time. Prior to the service, he asked people for memories and found that five themes emerged. One of the five themes was that she knew just the right time to drop an "f bomb". People saw that as showing her vulnerability, as well as a passionate way to share her frustration with a world and a system filled with inequities.

Brene Brown, author of "*The Power of Vulnerability,* says that she doesn't completely trust people who never swear. If a person is being vulnerable and honest, they probably will swear now and again with all the shit in the world and in our lives. I feel similarly. If a friend never swears around me, I wonder if they trust that I won't judge them. Or maybe they don't know me well enough to let themselves show vulnerability around me.

I have a female friend who is a great person whom I really admire. We have been close friends for almost thirty years. I didn't hear a swear word slip from her mouth for the first ten years we knew her. When she finally cut loose, it was the perfect situation and funny as heck. I laughed my head off. This made me like her even more, because I felt like she finally trusted Laketa and me enough to be herself.

I wonder if Mother Teresa, or Gandhi or Buddha ever swore. They seemed to always be so calm and mindful. They appear to have handled even horrible situations with tremendous inner peace. Sometimes I wonder if privately, or with one or two of their closest followers. they looked at a situation and said, "What the f***? Can you believe that? What a crummy world." If they did, I think I like them even more. After all, Simon Peter cussed and he's the rock of the Christian Church.

I'm aware that swearing too much is kind of juvenile. People who use the "f "word constantly need to develop a broader vocabulary and a better sense of perspective. Everything in their life can't possibly be so terrible that every sentence needs to include the "f" word.

However, I'm glad I finally gave myself the grace to toss out a few well-timed cuss words in the right situation. It has deepened my friendships by showing vulnerability and it's kind of a hoot, damn it! Oops, Cruz just came over, time to take it down a notch.

Where are my yearbooks?

I was looking for a couple of old photos to use in this book you are reading when I asked Laketa, "Where are my yearbooks?". She had no idea and let me know that wasn't really her problem. After tearing apart the shed on the deck for about fifteen minutes in the unbearable 72-degree heat, I remembered I had thrown them out when we moved. I figured I hadn't looked at them for about three decades, so I tossed 'em. What a dumb decision! It saved me about eleven inches wide and six inches high of space. Even Marie Kondo would say, "Ya know. I might keep those."

If you think 72 degrees isn't that hot, you probably don't live in NW Washington. We complain about the rain all year long and then the minute it gets warm, we gripe about that, too. Give us a break, it's not a dry heat!

Anyways, this made me question my sentimentality. Maybe I'm not sentimental enough. This kind of fits with my inability to let my guard down enough to form close attachments with people. Also, I don't remember a lot of my high school experience as the good old' days and who buys a college annual? Another insight for today.

If you are reading this and have some good high school or college photos of me, scan a couple over. I still have room on my Cloud! (What is a cloud, anyways?)

Who is this guy?
People often tell me what a positive and happy person I am. I suppose that's true. I'm a pretty content and happy-go-lucky guy. However, I also never really took time to self-reflect or be introspective and I'm finding that I'm not always as joyful as I appear on the outside. I faked it to one degree or another most of my life.

When I began toying with the idea of writing a book, I sent some of my writing to family and friends. Many were surprised when I shared reflections about being sad or angry. Everyone saw me as the funny and easygoing guy. A few people expressed that they didn't realize I had any sad memories or hard times. My response was, "I don't think I realized it either until I took the time to reflect and write."

I had a Sunday School teacher in junior high who was a college basketball coach. He told us that if we just had faith and lived a godly life, we would be the best athletes, workers, spouses, parents, and people. We would also have more than enough money, which was a nice bonus. I haven't been able to find that in the Bible recently, but I sure bought into those teachings as a kid. Looking back now, it doesn't seem like Jesus's top priority was ensuring we were all happy every minute of the day or finding the next party.

Very few tears found a way down my cheeks for about 35 years after I turned about four. I started tearing up a little more often after I had kids. I still didn't shed many tears though, and I'm not sure if more than a handful of people ever saw me cry. I don't remember even crying at funerals. I hope Lianne and Joel saw me cry now and again, but I'm not sure they did. Men were supposed to be strong in my day and that meant no crying. Mom used to say, "I'll give you something to cry about!"

The condo association we live in is about half Canadian. Recently, one of our Canadian neighbors asked me if everything in America needed to be a celebration, even funerals. That's a good question. I've generally tried to be positive, no matter the circumstances. I missed out on a lot in life by not letting myself be involved with grief or mourning. I closed off rooms in my heart and mind. Now I feel like the stuffed animal in the "Velveteen Rabbit". I'm a little beat up and lost an eye, but I've been loved and have lived a full life.

Jesus said blessed are those who mourn and weep. A funeral should offer people a chance to mourn and say goodbye, as well as to remember and celebrate. You not only lose the person; you also lose a part of yourself. After both my parents died, I not only lost my parents, I lost my role as a son.

I used to race to try to relieve the suffering and pain of those around me immediately when I saw someone else crying. Now I'm trying not to devalue their experience and I let them cry it out. Tears are not only ok; they can be good. I'm also learning not to devalue my own pain, even if others have it worse.

As John Green said, "When people try to minimize your pain, they are doing you a disservice. And when you try to minimize your own pain you are doing yourself a disservice. Don't do that. The truth is that it hurts because it's real. It hurts because it mattered. And that's an important thing to acknowledge to yourself."

"Tears … are not the mark of weakness, but of power. They are messengers of overwhelming grief and unspeakable love." Washington Irving

You should have listened to me thirty years ago
I am proud to say that I was decades ahead of my time for the Coronavirus pandemic of 2020. While the rest of the country was learning the importance of washing their hands this year, I was sitting back smugly patting myself on the back for figuring out the importance of handwashing in 1990. A human well ahead of my time. If people had followed my example thirty years ago, we wouldn't be in the mess we are in now!

I remember a beautiful spring day at Roosevelt, one of those Northwest Washington days that make all the rain worth it. I was strolling leisurely past the monkey bars when a first-grade girl walked up behind me, looped her arm through mine, looked up sweetly and said, "I love you, Mr. Morse". It was a touching moment for about three seconds before she proceeded to rub her very snotty nose all over my bare forearm. While inwardly my germaphobia immediately raced to a level 99.5, I outwardly remained calm and told her that I loved her, too. I managed to slowly extricate my arm, without tossing her twenty feet across the monkey bars.

I walked along and chatted pleasantly with her for a few minutes before informing her that I needed to get back to the office. I continued leisurely to the playground door and waved goodbye. The instant I was out of her sight, I speed walked down the hall like Bill Nye the Science Guy used to on "Almost Live", the Seattle version of Saturday Night Live. I passed wide-eyed kids while whispering, "I'm not running."

I raced to the sink in the workroom, rolled up my sleeves and started vigorously scrubbing away all the way up my arms. A teacher walked in and started laughing. She nicknamed me "The Surgeon", as these episodes occurred quite often. I'm glad that nickname didn't stick, although Laketa thinks I should have been a doctor every time she sees me write in cursive.

My handwashing obsession began my second year as principal in Westport. I was working about 65 hours a week and racing around at about 100 mph the whole time. This was before I learned the secret of walking slower and how to prioritize effectively. I'm sure I looked like a complete idiot. (No comment from my recent coworkers who thought I looked like an idiot to the day I retired. This is my book, not yours.)

It was May, and it was the second year in a row that I had a headache, sinus infection, and sore throat most of the time from mid-October until the end of the school year. I was sick and tired of being sick and tired. I decided if I couldn't figure this out, I would try the principal gig for one more year and then do something else. I wasn't willing to be sick for eight months every year for the next thirty years of my career.

I scheduled a doctor appointment. This is another moment I remember in clear detail, as if it happened yesterday. I can see the doctor's face and hear his voice. I was 34 years old and had only cried a few times since I was about four years old. Yet here I was, sobbing uncontrollably in the doctor's office. I couldn't continue like this.

He let me sob for a while and then gave me an idea to try for a few months. He told me to keep a water bottle on my person and drink all day long. I was tempted to spike it with a little rum, but alas, I decided not to do that. There were many days I wish I had! I was also told to vigorously scrub my hands at least once an hour, like a surgeon. It worked! I have been teased relentlessly about this habit for many years, but it has been well worth it! And now, for the icing on the cake, I get to bask in the knowledge that I was washing and fist-bumping decades years before y'all. Get on board, this train is leaving the station.

Life is long

Yeah, yeah, I know life is short. I've heard that a million times. However, in the last decade, I have concluded that life is also long. Like any profound truth, the opposite is also a profound truth. There were times in my life when I felt hopeless, but I worked through those times and discovered the sunshine again. I messed up over and over, but always had another chance to do better. I have friends who went through painful divorces and are now incredibly happy again. I know people who looked like they would never get their stuff together, and then one day, they got it together. When people are discouraged, I tell them that life is long. The sun will shine again. You will get another opportunity to rise again. I've come to realize that I always have time to become a better person, more human, more complete.

Even when everything in "my world" seemed to be going well, I would find a new way to screw something up. The problem was usually me, not my circumstances.

Ann Lamott tells a story about her six-year-old son getting his head stuck in a chair and saying, "I need help with me." Ann made that her motto and it would work perfectly for me, too. Nonetheless, life is long, and I usually got another chance through good times and bad.

I'm also discovering how interesting timing is. God's timing or the universe's timing is rarely the same timeframe as what I wanted. I want instant microwave solutions. I'm trying to be more patient, more gracious, and kinder to myself and others. I don't know what the future will hold, but so far, I know a lot of people who eventually came around, including myself.

Many students entered Roosevelt in kindergarten who already seemed destined for terrible life outcomes. Often, they made a few nice gains by the end of fifth grade, but it was not at all uncommon that we saw almost no improvement. However, one of us would often run into one of these kiddos in their late teens or early 20s. We were pleasantly surprised at how many of them had graduated from high school, were holding jobs, were happy, and appeared to genuinely love their own children. We always celebrated these serendipitous meetings. These chance encounters reminded us that you can't rush the growth process in human beings. It helped us be patient and take it one day at a time with the challenging students we were currently serving. You never know what will happen down the road, but in my experience, it's almost never what I expected.

Clint told me there is a saying in rehab that "this too will pass". The idea is to hold onto your values and your sobriety because the circumstances that feel overwhelming always pass. If you hold onto your better self during the most challenging times you won't live life with constant regrets and shame. The part of this saying that often gets overlooked is that when things are going well "that will pass" too. Don't expect things to go well all the time but be able and willing to be your best regardless of circumstances. When I'm discouraged, I strive to remember life is long. Good times will return again.

Make the coffee every morning

Laketa and I on post-retirement trip.

Watching Rom-Coms and going to an American high school, I had a warped view of what love was. If an alien watched American movies to learn about us, they might think love is only shown through grand gestures, and that romance is a "Where's Waldo" search of the one person out of the billions of people on earth who is your perfect soulmate. Laketa and I have been together forty years and there's a good chance we'll be together a few more. We learned that loving others through day by day small acts of kindness, not grand gestures, is the way to go. Every day gives us plenty of opportunity to love our significant others in a hundred ways. We don't have to wait until we can stand under a window with a boombox on our shoulders.

Each day brings the opportunity to care about the people we work with, our families and others we meet in our day to day journeys. Keith made the coffee most mornings in our office and whenever I said, "This coffee is good today", Keith answered, "It's made with love." When people came to the office, he always offered coffee immediately and took pride in how he made it.

Cheryl Strayed, author of "Wild" states it well, "Love is not so incomprehensible as you pretend, sweet pea. Love is the feeling we have for those we care deeply about and hold in high regard. It can be light as the hug we give a friend or heavy as the sacrifices we make for our children. It can be romantic, platonic, familial, fleeting, everlasting, conditional, unconditional, imbued with sorrow, stoked by sex, sullied by abuse, amplified by kindness, twisted by betrayal, deepened by time, darkened by difficulty, leavened by generosity, nourished by humor and "loaded with promises and commitments" that we may or may not want or keep."

Fred Rogers said," Love isn't a state of perfect caring. It's an active noun like struggle. To love someone is to strive to accept that person exactly the way he or she is, here and now. "

Enjoy your morning coffee.

Standing in the pouring rain holding a leash
I somehow talked my parents into getting a dog when I was in first grade even though they were never too interested in pets. Five wild kids were enough, I suppose. Tippy was in our family for about a year. He kept biting me. One day, one of my "friends" wouldn't let me out of a headlock no matter how hard I begged. Tippy latched onto his leg and held on a while, so dad gave him away to a family on a farm. At least that was his story, and he stuck with it.

Like dad, I never wanted a dog as an adult but Laketa and the kids always seemed to want one. We got a dog the first year we were married and still have one forty years later. Not the same dog of course. He would be like 50,000 years old in dog years, if my math is correct. This anecdote tells you everything you need to know about the shared decision-making model we use in our house.

Nonetheless, I ended up being the one to walk the dogs, take them to the vet, and do most everything else. Inevitably, I grew fond of every dog we had. In fact, some of my best hours each day are when I am outside with the dog. Many studies suggest that walking a dog leads to more happiness and a longer life. If so, I'll live a long time. Here are my three rules for walking the dog, or not.

1. Just walk the dog. Don't skip a day, don't make excuses. Get off that couch before you injure your shoulder. As Nike implores, "Just do it!"
2. Now and again, let the dog walk me. Stop and smell the flowers every time the dog stops to smell the urine. Let Tyson take the lead. Go wherever he wants to go. Enjoy the journey with no agenda about how far I am going, how many steps I'm getting on my app, etc. This helps me remember that I don't have to try to control everything in my life. One thing I discovered the hard way though, ... don't let Tyson drag me onto a stranger's porch. Let's just say that this lesson is better learned through reading a book than through experience, even though I made a new friend in the long run.
3. Take a walk without the dog sometimes. Relish the moment, look around, don't worry about the leash, just walk!

That's pretty much all I've learned about walking dogs. I'm not Cesar Millan.

What, me worry? ...Alfred E Neuman

Anxiety and depression are reaching epidemic levels in our society, and youth suicide rates are increasing. I was surprised how much time I spent on suicide protocols and concerns in my central office job. The current pandemic will probably only make anxiety and depression worse.

There are serious problems in our world, and we are more aware of these issues than we have ever been in the past. We have little control over the major issues. It's easy to get discouraged.

Statistically though, I am a member of the healthiest, safest, and wealthiest generation ever, yet our generation is arguably the most anxious and depressed ever. When will I learn to be content with what I have? Research suggests that if you have "enough, (The figure is usually between $75-$100k family income in America.) more money and possessions will not make you happier or less anxious.

The new findings in epigenetics (There are some excellent videos and articles on the internet if you aren't familiar with epigenetics.) suggest that many of our fears and trauma can be passed on genetically, as well as through our experiences. My father was always worried about money and even though I realize I have "enough", it has been challenging for me not to worry about money.

I'm not sure what the key is to reducing worry, but I have read some books that assisted me quite a bit. I enjoyed "Don't Sweat the Small Stuff" by Richard Carlson. "Buddha's Brain", by Rick Hanson and Richard Mendius was also helpful.

Anxiety for me seemed to be due to wanting to control everything. Having a mantra to repeat helps me slow the hamster wheel in my head. As a kid, I was taught that religions that had mantras were clearing our minds of conscious thought so that the devil could take over our minds. Now, I would pay $1000 to be able to clear my mind for just five minutes. My wheel just spins and spins like a 24-hour carnival ride. When I'm walking and the wheel keeps spinning, I've been using a mantra that Laketa showed me. It's from the old testament.

Be still and know that I am God
Be still and know that I am
Be still and know
Be still
Be

One of my initial learnings as a principal came when my first superintendent told me that I can't control *anything*. He suggested I let go of the illusion of control and try to influence teacher behavior, rather than trying to control behavior.

I didn't agree, so he followed up by asking me if I could control anything as a teacher, I foolishly let him know that there were at least a few behaviors I could control. (Huge mistake by a rookie principal.)

He asked me to name one thing I could control when I was teaching third grade. I ruminated for a minute and told him that when it was time for silent reading, every single student pulled out their book and read.

He replied, "Really.", picked up a book off his desk, leaned back in his chair, opened it up, and stared into the book. Touché, patron.

That was the inaugural lesson in my long quest of letting go of trying to control others and focusing more on my own behaviors. I can influence, but not control others. As a supervisor, I could even go down a path that might lead to the firing of someone, but I would never be able to make that person do anything they didn't want to do.

This quote by the writer, Elizabeth Gilbert, sums it up. "You are afraid of surrender because you don't want to lose control. But you never had control; all you had was anxiety."

When I was in a time of severe anxiety in the 90's, a friend taught me to take it one day at a time. He encouraged me to live out the day, say a prayer of thankfulness for that day as I retired for the night, and begin anew the next day. This wasn't rocket science. Other people had probably given me the same advice before. However, the timing was perfect, as I was at the point in my life where I was desperate for those words. I made a significant mental shift the same day and have tried to practice this ever since.

As I studied mindfulness, I realized that I needed to take it even further and try to live one minute (or one second) at a time. I can't control other people or many of my circumstances, but I can live in that moment. Or at least try!

Corrie Ten Boom says it well, "Worrying is carrying tomorrow's load with today's strength – carrying two days at once. It is moving into tomorrow ahead of time. Worrying does not empty tomorrow of its sorrow; it empties today of its strength."

While that makes perfect sense, it is much easier said than done. Worrying seems to be in my DNA. I have been a worrier since childhood. I worried about everything I was learning in church way more than my friends attending the same church. Most of the stuff I worried about just seemed to go in one ear and out the other for them.

I also worried about germs. My sisters would drop a handful of spaghetti noodles on the floor in front of me and exclaim loudly, "Oh no. We dropped those noodles on the floor. We would never waste them." With a smug look on their face, they would pick them up and stir them right into the middle of the rest of the spaghetti, as I watched in horror.

Clearing my mind and waiting turned out to be helpful. Some of my best decisions came to me only after I consciously tried to stop obsessing about the problem and started thinking about other things.

Religious leaders like Buddha and Jesus taught their followers not to worry. Jesus taught that worry won't change one hair on your head. While I have a long way to go in decreasing worry, I believe it is a priority that is worth my time!

Happiness in the time of Covid (Wouldn't that be a great title for a movie?)

The book of Ecclesiastes in the Old Testament says,
For everything there is a season, and a time for every matter under heaven:

[2] a time to be born, and a time to die;
a time to plant, and a time to pluck up what is planted;
[3] a time to kill, and a time to heal;
a time to break down, and a time to build up;
[4] a time to weep, and a time to laugh;
a time to mourn, and a time to dance;
[5] a time to cast away stones, and a time to gather stones together;
a time to embrace, and a time to refrain from embracing;
[6] a time to seek, and a time to lose;
a time to keep, and a time to cast away;
[7] a time to tear, and a time to sew;
a time to keep silence, and a time to speak;
[8] a time to love, and a time to hate;
a time for war, and a time for peace.

I have struggled with feeling a little guilty during the pandemic. We are both healthy right now, we get to see Cruz every day, we have food, and we can walk, bike, read, write, etc. Things are okay for us during a time when so many people have health and financial worries. In fact, I kind of enjoy the slower pace a little bit.

This isn't a new issue for me. Working in the schools I was exposed to many hurting kids and families. I saw homeless families, domestic abuse, and restraining orders. I understood the saying, "You never know what goes on behind closed doors.", with new ears. Even families that looked so solid often had many big issues.

About a month into my first principal job, I phoned my dad to tell him I wasn't sure I could do this job. Seeing so much poverty and pain every day was already affecting me after just a few weeks. I told Dad I didn't know how I lived on this planet for

34 years without realizing what was going on in the houses all around me. Dad listened, empathized, and continued to worry for a couple of months. It made me feel supported when he called a few times worried, although I also wished I hadn't mentioned it to him, as I hated to add to his burdens.

I didn't realize it at the time of this phone call, but I ended up being physically sick for much of my first two years as a principal. I think it was a combination of physical exhaustion, lack of sleep, stress, and heartbreaking sadness. These issues had always been there, but I had been living with my eyes closed. I didn't even realize how many kids were affected.

It's been hard at times not to feel guilty about the relatively easy life I have experienced so far, both materially and with my family of origin. I had some tough experiences in my childhood, but nothing remotely close to the trauma I was seeing daily in kids at school. I began to question whether it was "ok" to be happy when so many people are hungry, sick, poor, or living in violent situations.

As I write this reflection, it's about the fifth month of coronavirus social distancing, and all those thoughts are coming back to the surface again like a wave building and crashing on the beach. Is it ok for me to laugh at a tv show, enjoy a game online, enjoy Cruz, or laugh with a neighbor during a time when so many are experiencing loss of jobs, difficulty finding food, extreme physical illness and even death?

When I wonder if being happy is ok in a suffering world, I often harken back to a conversation in the 90's at Silver Beach. I was eating lunch with six to eight teachers. A massive winter wind and snowstorm was forecast to hit. Extreme cold and power outages were expected.

I mentioned to the group that Laketa, Lianne, Joel and I were all going to all sleep in the living room in front of the fireplace and make it an adventure for the kids. We were planning to read a ton, tell campfire stories, make s'mores, and play table games. I was looking forward to the opportunity to slow down and reconnect with my family, as I had been quite busy lately.

One of the people at the table told me that I was being incredibly selfish and should not be happy about this at all. "What about the homeless and the poor? What is wrong with you, Steve Morse?"

I pondered on that without responding for a while, as I had been struggling with the same issues around happiness myself for at least a decade. I thought she was probably right, and I should bemoan the coming storm and be miserable for a while.

After feeling terrible about myself for about ten minutes, I formed a few questions in my mind that helped shape my thinking for the rest of my life. I thought, "Will the storm miss our city if I am unhappy about it? Will it help the homeless if I am worried and stressed out for the four days of isolation? Will I be a more effective principal or parent if I spend the four days upset and worried or if I come back refreshed? Will there ever be a minute on this planet when someone somewhere isn't going through an atrocious situation? When will all the billions of people all be happy, healthy, warm, and full at the same time for even one second?"

I shared these contemplations with my tablemates. We ended up having a decent discussion and it reinforced my thinking that it's not only ok to be happy, but we damn well better grab any opportunity we have in our lives to experience joy, happiness and peace when it comes along. Savor joyful moments and hang on with both hands. Life will not always offer that opportunity.

Clint said that he has had to work through the same struggle over wealth. "Is it ok to enjoy a nice vacation and live in a luxury home when so many people don't have enough food?"

Clint and I came to the same conclusion on this. It's ok to be happy if it is tempered with thankfulness, empathy, and love for others. We should also be giving, sharing, and helping others when we have enough. While my elementary aged kids can enjoy the storm with Laketa and I, we should also pause and let them know that some people are out in this weather. It's an opportunity to teach them about giving and empathy and model giving money and ourselves during hard times.

Unfortunately, it appears that there will be a certain amount of pain in the world for some time to come. At any given moment, somewhere in the world, a family will be mourning the loss of a loved one, a child or partner will be experiencing abuse, and someone will be in a civil war. It's heartbreaking and I never want to allow myself to be ignorant or to skate through life with my eyes closed. I shouldn't grow weary or give up helping to make the world a better place. I don't want the immensity of pain to keep me from doing anything. We all just have to do the best we can to help those we can.

However, being sad and depressed isn't necessarily the best strategy for me. Succumbing to a numbing depression paralyzes me from even attempting to make a difference. I believe that there is a time for mourning and a time to experience peace and joy.

Like Mary Oliver says, "If you suddenly and unexpectedly feel joy, don't hesitate. Give in to it."

When it all seems overwhelming, I take a walk, play with Cruz, or play pickleball. I remind myself to let go of my guilt, find joy when and where I can, and serve others when and where I can.

I got hacked today
I learned a little bit about myself today and it wasn't pretty. Here I am writing a book about everything I've learned in my life over 64 years, and today, I reverted to my thirteen-year-old

self for about eight hours. I got so irritable and annoyed when I realized I'd been phished that my mind was reeling.

Mom's voice came back in a big way. I heard, "You're so stupid. How could you fall for that scam? Anyone would have known not to open that link.", about every ten minutes all day long.

I've been making steady progress on getting rid of that voice and one first world problem pops up and I'm back to square one. I made the decision to look at these eight hours as an aberration, and I'm putting myself back on track tomorrow. I don't know if it's true for anyone else, but I often handle the big things like cancer much more maturely than the little things.

I know no one is perfect and try to be graceful to others when they struggle, but good grief, I'm much harder on myself. I've got a lot of junk that I never seem to get past. I wasted about forty years in denial and really only began the deeper work about ten years ago. I wonder if I'll ever get much better about some of my deeper childhood stuff that pops up every now and again.

I was lamenting about a recent bout of FOMO today and wondering when in the heck I would ever get past my stuff when my nephew, Jordan, texted, "We carry our baggage to the grave. I keep thinking I'm going to outgrow my s***."

I laughed out loud and thought that was quite wise for a kid in his thirties. I don't think we ever completely outgrow our stuff, but I do believe that as I grow older and wiser, I get at least a little better at life in general. I think I have grown, but a few of the same areas seem to trip me up often, with no warning.

It's humbling writing a book. When I am writing about patience or unconditional love and snap at Laketa because she keeps interrupting my writing, I feel like such a fraud. When I am writing about the importance of family on the same day that I'm mad at a family member, the same. Writing exposed all of my hypocrisy and the distance I still need to travel on my life journey.

Clint claimed the same thing happened to him and he decided he might not even finish his second book, even though he is about 95 percent done. I feel exactly the same way today. If you are reading this though, it looks like I managed to keep going.

I stepped on a matchbox car in the middle of the night
"D'oh. That hurt like mad."

I stepped on a matchbox car in the middle of the night on my way to the bathroom and let out a yelp. And guess what, I didn't even get mad this time. In fact, I broke into a huge smile, thankful for the gift of our grandson, Cruz. We have wanted a grandchild for years. Now we just need to watch where we step.

Grab your backpack
For me, this is the beginning, not the end. My journey will not be completed by running faster or marching through the night. My destination will most likely be reached by letting go. Letting go of my need to always be right, to understand God and the universe perfectly, to control others, and for everyone to like me all the time, which will be the hardest of the four.

The hike will require me to continue to evolve and learn. Every time I wrote about something I learned, it felt like a misnomer, because I'm not sure I've really "learned" anything. I keep repeating the same lessons numerous times, and it often takes a whack upside the head to make it stick. If I write a second edition, I'm certain many of my thoughts will have changed and evolved. And that's a good thing. The trek will require new eyes to see what has been right in front of me all along.

As Marcel Proust said, "The real voyage of discovery consists not in seeking new lands but seeing with new eyes."

The isolation during the pandemic has been especially challenging the last several weeks. I have been telling myself "one day at a time" until things get a little better. I'm also hanging on to the quote from "The Best Exotic Marigold Hotel". "Everything will be all right in the end. If it's not all right, it's not the end." See you on the trail.

Not the end

ACKNOWLEDGEMENT

I mostly want to thank "you", the reader. We all have a story to tell and we all want to be heard. Thank you for hearing my story.

I would like to thank Laketa for her patience during writing, my siblings, Cheryl, Clint, and Laurel for reading my stories and giving me encouragement and feedback. Thanks to Dana Holgate, for his encouragement and for being in half the stories. A special thanks to Sandy Olsen and Denisa Anderson, who were avid readers and responders. Sandy also helped with the editing.

Thanks to my old college friend Mike Buzga who put in a lot of time helping edit and thanks to Terry Kaemingk, who was writing a book alongside of me and shared ideas.

Writing can be a solitary process and it helped me carry on when I received a word of encouragement as I plodded along. Thank you to the following people for reading samples along the way and sending me encouragement and suggestions; Doug Asbjornsen, Sue Asbjornsen, Tom Venable, Keith Schacht, Jessica Sankey, Robin Russell, Deborah Monroe, Terri McKee, Heidi Silvestri, Bob Winters, Lisa Peterson, Shelly Morse, Andrew Morse, Jordan Morse, Lillian Harris, Mariann Strachan, Kiersten Anderson Barr, Renee Kenady, Kara Burt, Megan Thygesen, Teresa Verde, Rex Allison, Elizabeth McKinley Boyle, and Kristen Ingman, Glynn Currie, Rod Buss, and David Flick.

I especially want to thank my dog, Tyson, as I thought of most of the ideas for this book while walking him through the rain, wind and snow several times a day. I raced home to write them down every time. He also models a rather good approach to daily living.

ABOUT THE AUTHOR

Steve Morse

Steve Morse lives in Birch Bay, Washington, with his wife, Laketa, and next door to his daughter, Lianne, and grandson Cruz. He worked in the public schools for 39.5 years, 24 as an elementary principal.

Made in the USA
Columbia, SC
23 September 2020